ROCKON

THE CRYSTAL HEALING HANDBOOK
FOR SPIRITUAL REBELS

—

KATE MANTELLO

ROCKPOOL

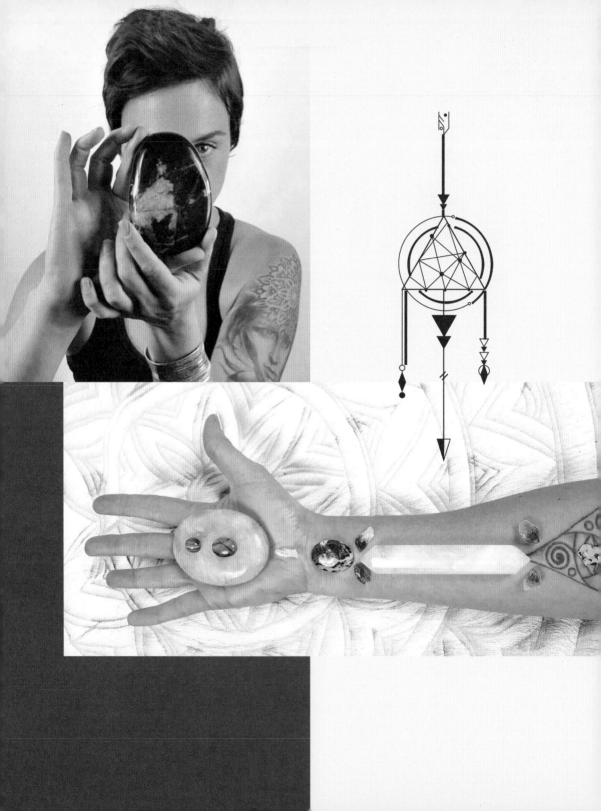

CONTENTS

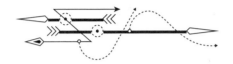

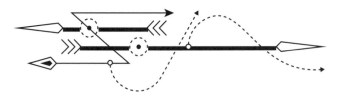

THIS BOOK IS DEDICATED TO
ROB, SOL AND EDIE
FOR TAMING THIS REBEL HEART.

———

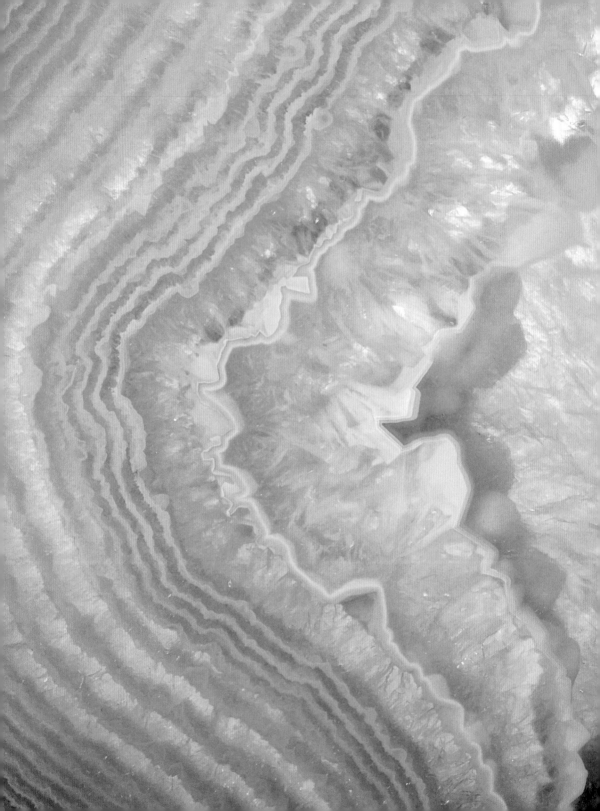

CRYSTALS ARE LIVING BEINGS AT
THE BEGINNING OF CREATION.

NIKOLA TESLA

CRYSTALS AND COMBAT BOOTS — THE BEGINNING

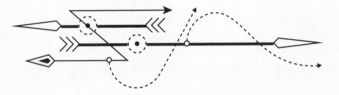

2007

I listened with half-interest to the middle-aged woman seated before me. She had long, wild red hair and was nattering on about the mystical powers of a blue crystal in her hand. Yawn. I wasn't sure how much longer I could keep my eyeballs from rolling back in my head, so I busied myself wondering what hair dye she used.

I felt a little out of place, sitting among this small group of eager (and slightly weird) healing students. I was here because I wanted to learn about energy healing after recently recovering from a traumatic spinal injury. This vibrational healing course had jumped out at me during a bleary-eyed, midnight internet search and, two months later, here I was.

As I looked around at all the purple tie-dye sitting in the room, I became aware of my black combat boots and jeans. I wondered if I really belonged here. I had never even held a crystal, let alone used it for healing. As far as I was concerned, it was just fluffy, spiritual 'woo-woo', generously sprinkled with fairy dust and unicorn farts.

So, when the course teacher began talking in reverent whispers about crystal devas and angel guides, I started looking for an escape route.

Seriously, get it together, people.

Don't get me wrong. It's not that I was a sceptic. I considered myself to be a deeply spiritual and open-minded person. It's just that going gaga over a handful of sparkly rocks really wasn't my thing.

I drew the line at rock-worshipping.

Of all the subjects included in the healing course, 'crystal healing' was the one I would happily have skipped. *Oh well*, I thought, *I'm here now.*

Fifteen minutes later and I was lying face-up on a massage table, a dozen or so colourful 'rocks' placed strategically along the length of my body.

At least I could enjoy a few minutes of shut-eye.

I wasn't expecting much, so I was surprised when strange things began to happen. First, I was cold. Then I was suddenly and uncomfortably hot. Flashing lights and colours began swirling before my closed eyes and I felt my mind slipping into what I can only describe as a kind of freefall.

Within a couple of minutes, I was in a deep state of visionary meditation. I felt as though a world of feeling, energy and heightened consciousness had been cracked open inside me, like a portal into my own core.

It was an acid trip without the acid.

When I finally sat up again after 20 (30? 60?) minutes, the first words out of my mouth were profound.

'Holy shit. I've *never* experienced anything like *that* before!'

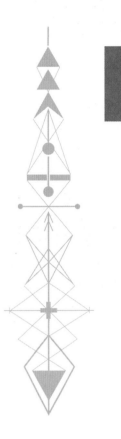

2021

That was 14 years ago. Not long after, I went on to study advanced crystal healing, transpersonal psychology, art therapy, Reiki, pranic energy healing and past life regression.

Despite my broad modality base, crystal healing has remained the mainstay of my practice. Crystals and I just *get* each other, and I find that my healing work is immeasurably more powerful when crystals are involved. Many people consider me something of a crystal healing expert, despite the fact I never sought this title, nor do I adorn myself in crystal jewellery (and, yes, I still wear black combat boots).

Now, with over a decade of professional experience and a global healing practitioner training institute under my belt, one thing has become 'crystal' clear: I may not have sought them out, but crystals sure chose me to be their spokesperson! I have taught crystal healing on stage at some of Australia's largest healing events and expos. My crystal healing courses are delivered across six continents and have been downloaded by over 20,000 people around the world. I've written extensively about crystal healing and have built social media platforms and online communities dedicated to this wonderful healing modality.

I am not here to tell you that meditating with a specific crystal will solve all your financial problems. Nor will keeping a Rose Quartz in your pocket magically manifest true love. True crystal healing requires more than the wave of a crystal wand.

It's about much more than New Age buzzwords like Aura Quartz and Tantric Twin. Crystal healing is about penetrating a person's deepest energetic layers to find the medicine they hold within. It's about real-world healing scenarios, like calming an anxious mind, supporting a mother through miscarriage or helping a partner overcome addiction. Crystal healing is about nurturing someone through emotional and psychological trauma like heartbreak and insecurity. It's about feeling all the feels, crying all the tears and being supported through your most raw and real human experiences, towards your ultimate healing.

A Spiritual Rebel understands this.

A Spiritual Rebel is a survivor and a soul searcher. She is a person who doesn't run from her pain, and who stands strong in her spirituality and dedication to her own personal evolution. A Spiritual Rebel does things her own way and is an active participant in her own healing journey. She might honour herself by meditating with an Amethyst crystal (while wearing angel wings) or by boxing bare-knuckled in a sparring ring.

Personally, I never resonated with the 'gentle approach'. I don't speak in breathless whispers and I am drawn to crystals that are rough and raw and more closely resemble dangerous weapons than pretty healing tools.

In the healing room, I like to take my clients deep, as quickly as possible. The crystal body layouts that you'll find in Part 3 of this book are a result of this work. When using the layouts, it is important to journey deeply, but respectfully. True healing can sometimes be an uncomfortable or emotional experience, so be gentle with yourself and those you are working with.

This book is the product of my 13 years on the front line, as a participant in and witness to the human healing journey. My experience with counselling, energy healing and transpersonal psychology has added a unique and specialised depth to my crystal healing work. I have held space for women who have lost babies,

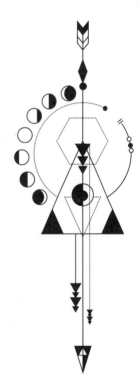

men who have been sexually abused and hopelessly lost souls who feel they have nothing left to live for. I have had my heart melted a hundred times by the raw force of love and heartbreak and I have witnessed transformations that no one thought possible.

This means I do things a bit differently. My crystal healing techniques have been developed in real healing sessions with real clients. Some of my techniques may even be quite radical, compared with what you may be familiar with.

You see, crystal healing is a journey. And like any journey, healing has a beginning, a middle and a destination. I didn't say an 'end', because healing is like evolution – there is no finite finish-line. Even a healed broken bone will continue to hold the physical

and energetic scars of its trauma indefinitely. The human body and soul are constantly changing landscapes, and each new realisation about yourself will uncover new opportunities for healing and transformation.

So, I can't offer you a magical crystal fix to fast-track you to an imaginary 'end' or finish-line. What I can offer you is a way to harness the power of crystals to support, facilitate and deepen your healing journey. I can offer you the knowledge and skills you will need to work with crystal energy in your own home or healing practice and experience its power for yourself. In short, I am offering you a way to take back ownership of your own healing experience, using one of nature's most incredible gifts, combined with the knowledge I can share from over a decade of professional healing experience.

It is not my intention to regurgitate the same crystal healing information that you may have read a hundred times over. Rather, my goal is to provide you with a practical, unique and hands-on crystal healing guide that will help enhance the lives of you, your loved ones and your clients.

This is the book I wish I'd had when I was beginning my crystal healing journey. It is for all you Spiritual Rebels out there who are courageous enough to journey beyond the ordinary and into the realm of the extraordinary. Whether you are beginner or expert, mystic or medic, if you have an open heart and you love crystals, then this book is for you.

Now, I invite you to take my hand and plunge in, fearless.

Enjoy the journey.

Kate Mantello

PART

1

A REBEL'S INTRODUCTION TO CRYSTAL HEALING

———

THE FOUNDATIONS OF CRYSTAL HEALING

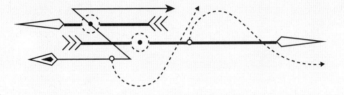

CRYSTAL HEALING 101 — AN INTRODUCTION

Crystal healing (also known as crystal therapy or gemstone healing) is the practice of using crystals, minerals and precious metals on people or animals to bring about healing and to enhance wellness in the physical and energetic body. While this all sounds impossibly 'New Age', the complete opposite is true: crystal healing is one of the oldest natural healing modalities known to humanity. Almost all the great and ancient civilisations (including the Hebrews, Mayans, Egyptians and Aztecs) incorporated sacred stones into their religious, philosophical and healing practices. Crystals have been discovered inside Egyptian burial chambers and precious stones found in ancient tribal jewellery, amulets, garments and records of sacred ceremonies.

In modern culture, we continue to perpetuate the idea that crystals hold supernatural powers through films such as *The Dark Crystal* (Amethyst), *Moana*

(Jade / Greenstone), *Indiana Jones and the Kingdom of the Crystal Skull* (Quartz), *Superman* (Kryptonite) and *Game of Thrones* (Obsidian / Dragon's Glass), and books like *The Alchemist* by Paulo Coelho and *Harry Potter and the Philosopher's Stone* by J. K. Rowling, both of which feature magical stones as their focal point.

In terms of practical and therapeutic application, crystal healing has massively increased in popularity in recent years and is now a professionally recognised healing modality in most parts of the developed world. Unlike many other healing modalities, crystal therapy involves no body manipulation, no application of oils or creams and no ingestion of medications or supplements (or other potentially harmful substances), and carries almost zero risk of side-effects or injury. It is an extremely subtle and enjoyable healing modality that can be used just as effectively to help someone through emotional or mental imbalance (such as a marriage break-up or anxiety), as to support someone through a physical injury or illness.

Most people would be surprised to learn that crystal healing is already deeply infused into our daily life. For example, most water filters contain a combination of specific minerals to cleanse and purify water. Baltic Amber necklaces have become popular for young children because they can help to relieve teething pain. Microchip and LCD technologies would not be possible without harnessing the energetic properties of Clear Quartz crystals (more on this later; see page 44).

This book is your one-stop guide to crystal healing. Not only will you learn about the scientific and metaphysical aspects of crystal healing, but you will learn the art of *applied* crystal healing: how to use crystals with intention and skill on the physical body to promote healing and wellness for life's most common health situations and challenges.

The energy of each person is completely unique, as is the energy of each individual crystal. The art of applied crystal healing is the practice of intentionally uniting these two energies (human and crystal) to create a

vibrational shift throughout the entire body — bringing alignment, cleansing, balance, release and healing to all levels of being.

You do not need a degree or professional training to benefit from the healing energies of crystals. While there *is* a lot of technique and knowledge involved in applied crystal healing (which we will cover in Parts 2 and 3 of this book), all you really need to get started are a couple of healing crystals and an open mind.

Are you ready?

NOT ALL ROCKS ARE CREATED EQUAL — CRYSTAL TYPES AND THEIR USES

There are hundreds of different crystals and stones used in crystal healing. Many are cheap and readily available. Some, like diamonds, are expensive and rare.

Some are sparkly and gorgeous. Others have curious, mystical names like Aura Quartz, Lemurian Seed and Isis Crystal. And some crystals are so impossibly colourful that you might be easily dazzled into thinking they are other-worldly.

A word of advice.

In the world of crystals and minerals, pretty does not equal powerful. A fancy name does not guarantee performance. And if the crystal's shade of fluorescent pink and purple matches a 1980s aerobics sweatband, then you can be sure it has been dyed (that's not to say it won't make an eye-catching piece of crystal bling, though!). When choosing crystals for healing purposes, it is best to select natural stones that have not been heat-treated or artificially dyed.

Shape is not really of any consequence, as both natural and shaped stones have their different uses. What is vitally important, however, is that you truly *resonate* with the stones you work with.

There are three important things to consider when selecting and purchasing crystals for healing:

◊ Type – Does the crystal have appropriate healing properties for its chosen purpose?

◊ Shape – Is the crystal natural, shaped or cut and what will it feel like to work with?

◊ Energetic vibe – How does the crystal feel energetically to you?

In this section of the book, we will look at the first two points but not the third, because that one is something only you can decide for yourself.

PURCHASING CRYSTALS

When purchasing your crystals, always be sure to source them from reputable and ethical sellers and wholesalers. I prefer to select my crystals in-person as I am very tactile and the physical contact is important for me to sense the crystal's energy. You may not need this level of contact to choose a crystal, or you may live in a remote area, so purchasing online may be more convenient for you. That's absolutely fine too! Either way, be sure that you trust the seller and their pieces are high quality. I found it difficult to source healing stones in my preferred size, shape and quality, which is why I opened my own online crystal store for dedicated crystal healers. (To purchase the same type of crystals that I work with, please visit evolvehealing.net/shop.)

DIFFERENT CRYSTAL TYPES

Following are the different crystals featured in this book – these are the crystals I have used the most in my crystal healing career. You may love working with crystals that are not mentioned in this book. This is perfectly fine, of course; however, if you are re-creating the crystal body layouts in Part 3, then it is best to use the correct stones wherever possible. ('Crystal body layout' is the term I use to describe a strategic arrangement of crystals on the body for a specific healing outcome. You might also be familiar with the phrase 'crystal body grid', which means the same thing.)

I've also included mention of which chakra the crystal relates to. The word 'chakra' means 'wheel' in Hindi and the idea that the chakras are energy centres within the human body was first linked to the Vedas, a collection of ancient Indian scriptures dated somewhere between 1700 BCE and 500 BCE. Each chakra forms a powerful centre of spinning prana, or life-force energy, which fuels the human energetic system. You'll read more about the chakras in 'Crystal healing and the chakras' on page 59.

If you do find yourself needing to substitute any of the crystals, then please be sure to use stones of a similar colour, shape and healing application for best results (read more about substituting crystals on page 104).

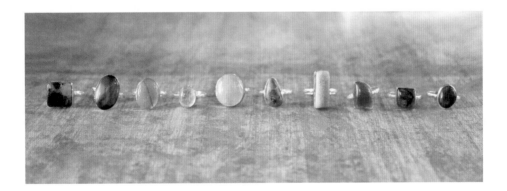

CRYSTAL	APPEARANCE	CHAKRA	HEALING PROPERTIES AND USES
AMAZONITE		Throat Heart	• Calms and soothes • Cleanses • Relieves muscle tension • Communication • Emotional balance
AMBER		Solar Plexus Sacral	• Cleanses • Energises • Soothes inflammation • Recharges • Digestive health
AMETHYST		Crown Third Eye	• Cleanses and purifies • Heals addiction • Spiritual growth • Meditation • Inner peace
AMETRINE		Crown Third Eye Solar Plexus Sacral	• Cleanses and purifies • Removes blockages • Abundance • Positivity • Health
AQUAMARINE		Third Eye Throat Heart	• Reduces stress • Cleanses • Protects • Balances • Clarity
AZURITE		Third Eye Throat	• Alleviates pain • Intuition and psychic development • Past life regression • Astral travel • New belief systems
BLOODSTONE		Heart Sacral Root	• Cleanses and detoxifies • Unblocks • Grounds and stabilises • Heals immune and circulatory systems • Emotional balance

CRYSTAL	APPEARANCE	CHAKRA	HEALING PROPERTIES AND USES
BLUE LACE AGATE		Throat	- Elicits truth - Heals sore throat - Communication - Personal expression - Thyroid health
CALCITE		All, depending on colour of stone	- Heals - Cleanses - Aligns - Personal growth and expansion - Meditation
CARNELIAN		Sacral Root	- Cleanses and detoxifies - Unblocks - Healthy metabolism - Sexual and reproductive health - Energy and vitality
CELESTITE		Higher Crown Crown	- Calms and sedates - Alleviates pain - Enhances psychic vision - Dreamwork - Meditation
CHAROITE		Crown Third Eye	- Alleviates stress and worry - Transforms negative to positive - Calms the mind - Spiritual growth - Transformation
CHIASTOLITE		Heart Root Earth	- Grounds - Aids letting go - New beginnings - Transformation - New direction and 'crossroads'
CHRYSOCOLLA		Crown Third Eye Throat Heart	- Calms and soothes - Serenity and tranquillity - Emotional healing - Self-awareness - Communication

CRYSTAL	APPEARANCE	CHAKRA	HEALING PROPERTIES AND USES
CHRYSOPRASE		Throat Heart Solar Plexus	• Relaxes • Calms and soothes • Cools inflammation • Channels energy • Abundance
CITRINE		Crown Solar Plexus Sacral	• Cleanses • Regenerates and energises • Joy and positivity • Heals addiction • Inspiration and creativity
COPPER		All, especially: Solar Plexus Sacral	• Energises • Amplifies • Grounds • Alleviates pain • Abundance
EMERALD		Heart Solar Plexus	• Cleanses • Heals emotions and heart • Loyalty and trust • Recovery after illness • Patience
FIRE AGATE (OR ORANGE AGATE)		Solar Plexus Sacral Root	• Protects • Strengthens • Sexual energy • Life-force energy • Vitality
FLUORITE		All, depending on colour of stone	• Heals and cleanses • Learning • New patterns and beliefs • Mental clarity • Psychic protection
GARNET		Third Eye Heart Root	• Opens awareness • Regenerates lower organs • Past life regression • Kundalini energy • Fertility and sexual health

CRYSTAL	APPEARANCE	CHAKRA	HEALING PROPERTIES AND USES
GREEN AVENTURINE		Heart	<ul><li>Soothes emotional pain</li><li>Reduces fever</li><li>Alleviates inflammation</li><li>Emotional balance</li><li>Heart, lungs and adrenals</li></ul>
HEMATITE		Root Earth	<ul><li>Grounds</li><li>Cleanses and detoxifies</li><li>Mental clarity</li><li>Focus and determination</li><li>Magnetic</li></ul>
IOLITE		Crown Third Eye	<ul><li>Connects to spirit realms</li><li>Shamanic practice</li><li>Higher purpose</li><li>Astral travel</li><li>Psychic vision</li></ul>
JASPER		All, depending on colour of stone	<ul><li>Grounds and stabilises</li><li>Balances</li><li>Unblocks</li><li>Harmonises spirit and physical</li><li>Lower and digestive organs</li></ul>
KUNZITE		Higher Crown Crown Third Eye Throat Heart	<ul><li>Aligns emotional energy</li><li>Raises heart–awareness</li><li>High vibrational</li><li>Spiritual development</li><li>Intuition and intellect</li></ul>
KYANITE (BLUE)		All, especially: Third Eye Throat	<ul><li>Aligns all chakras</li><li>Heals spine</li><li>Truth and integrity</li><li>Meditation</li><li>Overcoming fear</li></ul>
LABRADORITE		Crown Third Eye Throat Heart Solar Plexus	<ul><li>Awakens psychic energy</li><li>Supports menopause</li><li>Understanding and wisdom</li><li>Transformation</li><li>Divine feminine</li></ul>

CRYSTAL	APPEARANCE	CHAKRA	HEALING PROPERTIES AND USES
LAPIS LAZULI		Third Eye Throat	- Cools and soothes - Meditation - Truth-seeking and communication - Psychic protection - Throat and thyroid
LARIMAR		Third Eye Throat Heart	- Harmonises dualities within - Balances - Cleanses aura and energy - Removes negativity - Communication
LEPIDOLITE		Crown Third Eye Heart	- Unblocks mentally and spiritually - Heals physical body - Reconciles past with present - Alleviates depression - Release from being 'stuck'
MALACHITE		Heart Solar Plexus	- Protects physically and spiritually - Clears electromagnetic debris - Unblocks heart and emotions - Highlights trauma - Travel
MOLDAVITE		All, especially: Third Eye Throat Heart	- Activates all chakras - Speeds up evolution - Spiritual ascension - Cosmic and earth energy - Unlimited possibility
MOONSTONE		Higher Crown Crown Third Eye Root	- Connects to nature - Calms and sedates - Spiritual awareness - Sleep - Fertility (women)
OPAL		All, especially: Heart	- Grounds - Balances emotions - Amplifies - Absorbs negative energy - Loyalty and romance

CRYSTAL	APPEARANCE	CHAKRA	HEALING PROPERTIES AND USES
ORTHOCERAS		Root Earth	• Grounds • Connects to ancestral history • Reconciles the past • Aligns spine • Mental focus
PYRITE		Solar Plexus Sacral	• Energises • Self-confidence • Personal power • Abundance • Success
QUARTZ (CLEAR)		All, especially: Higher Crown Crown	• Heals • Cleanses • Clarity • Spiritual growth • Manifestation
RHODOCHROSITE		Heart	• Heals emotional trauma • Self-acceptance • Passion • Stimulates libido • Deep, spiritual love
RHODONITE		Heart	• Heals emotional trauma • Heals physical trauma • Balances emotions • Opens heart and emotions • Forgiveness
RUBY ZOISITE		Heart	• Emotional balance • Self-expression • Motivation • Abundance • Recovery after illness
ROSE QUARTZ		Heart	• Deep, spiritual love • Compassion • Forgiveness • Self-acceptance • Heart health

CRYSTAL	APPEARANCE	CHAKRA	HEALING PROPERTIES AND USES
SELENITE		All, especially: Higher Crown Crown	• Clears and repels negativity • Cleanses aura and environment • Psychic protection • Meditation • Life purpose
SHIVA LINGAM		Root Earth	• Grounds • Divine masculine energy • Fertility and sexual health • Virility • Stamina
SMOKY QUARTZ		All, especially: Root Earth	• Grounds • Regenerates and energises • Cleanses • Protects • Alleviates stress and depression
SODALITE		Third Eye Throat	• Relieves anxiety • Calms panic attacks • Mental clarity • Communication • Immune system and throat health
SUGILITE		Crown Third Eye Heart	• Opens heart and mind • Illuminates truth • Sense of belonging • Universal love • Wisdom
SUNSTONE		Solar Plexus Sacral	• Radiates joy • Releases doubt and fear • Alleviates depression • Abundance • Positivity and optimism
TIGER'S EYE		Solar Plexus Sacral Root Earth	• Protects against harm and evil • Aligns • Grounds • Harmonises dualities • Personal power and success

CRYSTAL	APPEARANCE	CHAKRA	HEALING PROPERTIES AND USES
TIGER'S IRON		Solar Plexus Sacral Root Earth	• Nourishes blood • Grounds • Motivates • Energises • Vitality
TOURMALINE		All, depending on colour of stone	• Unblocks • Aligns • Cleanses • Highlights self-limitations • Raises consciousness
TURQUOISE		Third Eye Throat Heart	• Purifies and protects • Alleviates depression • Communication • Positive relationships • Throat and immune system
WATERMELON TOURMALINE		Heart	• Breaks old patterns • Reduces negative thinking • Releases emotional trauma • New ways • Emotional support

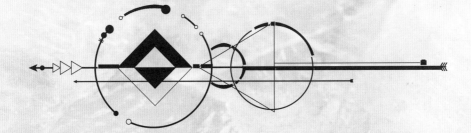

DIFFERENT CRYSTAL SHAPES

TUMBLED STONES

The most commonly recognised crystal shape is probably that of the humble tumbled crystal. You have surely admired at some point the rainbow of assorted tumbled crystals available at most crystal and New Age retail stores. Tumbled crystals are a great starting point for crystal collectors. They are inexpensive, come in a great range and are usually the real deal. This makes them a popular choice for crystal healing beginners. But what you might not know is that they can be quite awkward and impractical for most serious crystal healing bodywork.

Bodies, of course, come in an infinite range of shapes, sizes and curves. Commercially popular tumbled stones may look pretty in a bowl, but they tend to misbehave as soon as they are placed on a living, breathing, rounded human body. Strategically placed tumbled crystals look fab on an Instagram model, but the reality is one cough or sneeze and suddenly it's raining crystals! This is why I always prefer larger, flatter stones (such as palm stones or cabochons) for crystal bodywork.

CABOCHONS AND WORRY STONES

A cabochon is a crystal that has been cut into an oval or circle shape that is flat on one side and curved and polished on the other. Because they are cut to exact and specific sizes, cabochon crystals are popular with those who like symmetry and prefer their crystals to be uniform shapes and sizes. Worry stones are similar in that they come in uniform oval shapes; however, the back of the crystal has been hollowed out slightly to allow your thumb to comfortably sit in the dip.

Cabochons and worry stones are a preferred crystal type in crystal healing because they sit flat against the body and are usually of a better quality than tumbled crystals.

FLAT STONES AND PALM STONES

Flat stones (also known as palm stones) are larger than standard tumbled stones and have been roughly polished and shaped into discs. They are not precisely cut like cabochons, so they do vary in size and are therefore usually a cheaper option. They are also a preferred crystal choice for bodywork because they do not roll around.

ROUGH OR NATURAL STONES

A rough or natural stone is one that has not been cut, polished or shaped, but is in its natural, raw form. Sometimes a stone may be partially natural and have only one side cut and polished. Natural stones can be used as highly effective healing tools; however, there are some important factors to consider when selecting rough crystals for bodywork.

Some crystals (such as Malachite) and other metals, minerals and fossils used in crystal healing contain toxic particles that can cause skin rash and irritation. When a crystal is polished, the surface of the crystal is smoothed and sealed, becoming almost completely non-porous. This means that none of the particles can escape the crystal and it is less likely to absorb moisture or be damaged. However, rough stones are much more porous, meaning particles easily become dislodged and the stone is more susceptible to damage from moisture or friction (from sweaty hands or rubbing against other stones, for example).

For this reason, I prefer to keep my natural stones as display pieces and only work with a limited number of natural stones on the body.

CRYSTAL SHAPES	WHY YOU'LL LOVE THEM	THINK ABOUT IT
Tumbled	• Affordable • Large variety • Readily available	• Low quality • Irregular sizes • Roll off the body
Cabochon	• Uniform size • Higher quality • Do not roll off the body	• More expensive • Less available • Limited variety
Flat/Palm	• Affordable • Do not roll off the body • Good quality	• Less available • Limited variety • Some size variance
Rough/Natural	• Affordable • Natural • Easier to get larger sizes	• Irregular shapes and sizes • Potentially harmful dust • More easily damaged

CRYSTAL POINTS

Small crystal points (sometimes called 'chargers') are formed naturally in some types of crystal (such as Amethyst and Quartz) but can be created through intentional shaping from almost all types of stone. Unlike tumbled or flat stones, crystal points are placed strategically on and around the body in a grid-like design to enhance and direct the flow of energy. I prefer small, naturally formed Clear Quartz, Amethyst and Citrine points when it comes to crystal bodywork.

Although crystal points are not essential to your healing practice, they feature heavily in the layouts you'll find in Part 3 because they are an important part of my crystal healing technique. Crystal points (especially Clear Quartz points) have the ability to channel energy and enhance the effect of other stones in a crystal body layout.

PSYCHIC SURGERY

Psychic surgery is a term used to describe very precise energy healing work, in which the practitioner visualises performing surgery on a client but does not penetrate the skin. For example, you may use laser wands to penetrate a person's energy field and perform actions of cutting open tissue, separating muscles and stitching without any physical contact with the client. Psychic surgery is very advanced healing work and is not recommended for beginners.

CRYSTAL WANDS

A crystal wand is a crystal that has been cut and shaped or has naturally formed into a long, thin point. Crystal wands are used to perform concentrated energy work such as aura cleansing, chakra charging, psychic surgery (see above) and more. They are often the most important tool in a crystal healer's kit.

Unlike tumbled and flat stones, which are placed directly on the body, wands are held above the body and are used dynamically throughout a crystal healing session to channel and direct energy.

Most wands work by funnelling energy through a pointed tip.

This makes them excellent for more precise healing work. In the case of Clear Quartz, which is piezoelectric (more on this later; see page 44), the energetic charge is amplified and concentrated into a laser-like beam out of the tip of the wand.

In a single-tipped wand (also known as single-terminated), the concentrated beam of energy will flow in the direction the wand is pointed. For example, if we want to direct healing energy towards the body, then we point the wand tip towards the body. To carry negative energy away from the body, we face the wand point away from the body. Some wands have points at both ends (known as double-terminated), which means that energy is funnelled in both directions simultaneously.

There are colourful wands, natural wands, laser wands and Vogel wands. There are wands for individual chakras, massage wands and wonderfully twisted wands for self-pleasuring.

VOGEL WAND

Vogel wands are very powerful healing wands that were first created by Marcel Vogel (1917–1991), who was a research scientist for IBM for 27 years. Later in his career, Vogel became interested in the unique properties of Quartz crystal, including its unique cellular structure and piezoelectric properties. Based on his research, he created the first Vogel wand, which was precisely cut to maximise and harness the unique energetic properties of Quartz. There are several features that a wand must have to be a true 'Vogel', one of which is that the wide end of the wand must be faceted to form an internal angle of 51 degrees, 51 minutes and 51 seconds. This is essentially the same angle as the sides of the Great Pyramid of Giza.

If you are new to crystal healing and you are not sure which wand to start with, I recommend investing in a single-terminated Clear Quartz wand (such as a Lemurian Laser wand). A good quality Clear Quartz wand can be used at all chakras and for all types of healing, and is the most versatile of healing wands.

CRYSTAL PENDULUMS

A crystal pendulum is a crystal that has been shaped into a well-balanced point and hangs from the end of a short chain. Pendulums are popular in crystal healing and are widely available at most crystal retail stores.

It is fascinating to learn that pendulums (though not necessarily made from crystal) have a rich and documented history and are used in many types of technologies, from grandfather clocks to scientific instruments such as accelerometers and seismometers. They have even been used by pendulum experts (known as dowsers) working for armies and governments to source water or bombs in foreign territories. In the United States, both George Smith Patton (Army General during the Second World War) and Robert McNamara (Secretary of Defense during the Vietnam War) employed professional dowsers to locate hidden tunnels, unexploded mines and ammunition dumps.

Like wands, crystal pendulums are held above the body and are used more dynamically in a crystal healing session. They work by responding to subtle vibrational, magnetic and energetic frequencies in a person's aura (see next page), which may otherwise be undetectable by hand. This makes them excellent for use across a range of intuitive, investigative and diagnostic techniques in crystal healing. This includes chakra cleansing, aura 'sweeping', locating energetic blockage and answering specific questions. I once knew a woman who even took her crystal pendulum shopping – she would hold it over the fresh produce to select the most high-vibe vegetables!

AURA

The term 'aura' describes the part of our energetic body that extends out beyond the physical layers of our skin. Some people have the ability to see auras, and Kirlian photography can actually capture an image of a person's aura by photographing the electrical discharges that surround the physical body. Although there are no physical nerve endings in the aura, you can often sense when a person is touching or entering your auric space. For example, you might feel claustrophobic if a person is standing too close, or your skin might prickle where someone is pointing their finger at you.

I personally do not work with pendulums because I receive a lot of energetic information through my hands. I find that a pendulum's long chain disrupts the strength and flow of the energy between my client's body and my hand and dulls the information I am receiving. However, pendulums are extremely popular with many professional crystal healing practitioners and you may find your experience working with them is different from mine. You might even like to try incorporating a pendulum into the crystal body layouts in Part 3.

When selecting a crystal pendulum, choose intuitively which one will work best for you. You may like to keep a selection of crystal pendulums on hand for working on different areas of the body or for different body layouts. For example, a Rose Quartz pendulum would be perfect for understanding matters of the heart, while a Sodalite pendulum would work wonders at the throat.

OTHER CRYSTAL SHAPES

There are many other different crystal forms such as blades, obelisks, geodes, pyramids, master crystals and spheres (to name a few). However, there is no 'one size fits all' with crystal healing, because each person's energetic imprint is unique. Therefore, the most important aspect of working effectively and authentically with crystals is to honour what resonates with *you*. This can be as simple as just holding a crystal and feeling the shape of it in your hands. You might like to close your eyes and tune in to its temperature, texture and energetic vibe. If it feels good, then it's probably the right crystal for you.

As a Spiritual Rebel, you should always listen to your intuition and don't get too stuck on following the 'rules' if they do not resonate with you. Honouring yourself authentically is the key to maximising your amazing and unique journey of spiritual growth.

LOVE YOUR CRYSTALS AND THEY'LL LOVE YOU BACK — CRYSTAL CARE

If you are a crystal lover, then you know how special each of your crystals can become to you. Crystals are just like a pet or a house plant – if you love them, they'll love you back!

Each crystal has its own unique 'personality' and consciousness, and it is easy to become deeply connected to your special stones. I have a large Amethyst cluster beside my bed, and I love seeing the individual little crystals twinkle in the warm light of my lamp each evening. I feel relaxed just looking at it, and often feel like it is watching over me as I sleep.

Just like pets and plants need nutrients and care, so do crystals. Crystals are evolving, energetic beings. Any person who owns a self-healed crystal (see next page) can attest to that. The more time and energy you put into your crystals, the more you will receive back from them energetically.

One of the reasons why crystals are such effective healing tools is their ability to soak up negative energy. This is great if you

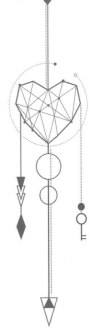

are having a bad day and can 'lift' some of your energetic funk by sweeping through your aura with a crystal. But just like we need a bath at the end of the day to wash away physical dirt, crystals need to be cleansed to help them release all the energetic gunk they absorb from their environment. This means that one of the most important aspects of crystal care is knowing how and when to cleanse your crystals.

Other important aspects of good crystal care are knowing how to safely store and transport your crystals, and how to connect (or attune) to your healing stones energetically.

CRYSTAL-TO-CRYSTAL CLEANSE

While most crystals require energetic cleansing after each use, some crystals (such as Citrine and Selenite) are so high-vibe that they do not absorb any negative energy and can cleanse other crystals through physical contact with them.

SELF-HEALED CRYSTAL

Most people believe that crystals are 'dead' objects that never change. However, some crystals (like Quartz) continue to grow new crystals over time. A crystal that has been broken and has grown a layer of new crystals at the site of the break is called a self-healed crystal. Sometimes a crystal can self-heal very quickly and may even grow new crystals over a period of a few short years. Self-healed crystals are excellent for reminding us that we all have the capacity to heal ourselves, no matter how large the trauma.

Simply place your crystal to be cleansed on top of a Citrine cluster, or in a cotton bag with tumbled Citrine or Selenite, and leave for at least 10 minutes. Speed up or amplify the cleanse process by placing the crystals in direct sunlight, or incorporating Reiki or visualisation.

VISUALISATION

This is a great option for those who can focus their mind with powerful intent. Place the crystal to be cleansed on a white cloth or natural surface (such as a bamboo mat). Focus your eyes and mind on the crystal and visualise a beam of white or golden light shining through the stone, releasing any negative energy. You might also like to hold your hands over the stone and visualise healing energy flowing out through your palms into the crystal. Sit with this intention for approximately a minute, or until the crystal seems lighter.

WATER BATH

Water has long been used in spiritual and ritualistic bathing ceremonies to wash away dark and negative energies (think about baptism, for instance). Crystals can also be cleansed with clean running water, but I do not recommend this method for most healing crystals.

Unless the stone is of a hard structure and is thoroughly polished, there is a significant chance that immersing it in water will damage or erode its surface. This is especially true of rough and raw crystals and crystals ending in 'ite' (such as Malachite, Selenite and Azurite). The mineral composition of these stones makes them much more likely to dissolve or be damaged in water. For this reason, it is best to cleanse your crystals using one of the other methods outlined in this section, especially if you are a beginner.

MOON CLEANSE AND SUN BATH

Crystals absolutely love celestial energy! At least a couple of times per year, I recommend placing your crystals out under a full moon overnight, preferably in a geometric grid for the best energy flow. They will soak up all that lunar energy and release any negative energy they have been storing. The sun and moon also act like energetic 'chargers' – recharging your crystals and restoring all their vitality and power.

Be sure to handle your crystals carefully for a couple of days after a full moon cleanse. The energetic vibration of the crystal will be at its maximum and this can even lead to cracking in some very high-vibe crystals. I usually carry my crystals inside very carefully after a moon cleanse and place them in an out-of-the-way place for a couple of days. This allows the crystals time to fully integrate the lunar energy and for the vibration to settle. The crystals will then be ready for use.

SMUDGING

Smudging is my go-to method for crystal cleansing because it is fast, effective and safe for all crystals, and leaves the space smelling beautiful afterwards! Smudging is an ancient practice where smoke is used from burning sacred leaves, grass, wood chips or plant resin to energetically cleanse a space or person. Not only is smoke highly effective in killing airborne bacteria and reducing toxins, but, energetically speaking, it's a wonderful cleanser.

Depending on where you come from, sweetgrass, white sage, lavender, palo santo and myrrh are all popular choices for smudging. A smudge cleanse can be intensified by visualising negative energy being lifted out and carried away as the smoke curls around the crystal.

STORING AND TRANSPORTING CRYSTALS

Crystals are 100 per cent organic substances that were birthed deep in the Earth. So, it only makes sense that they remain at their energetic best when they are stored in a container made from an equally natural substance.

Storage containers such as cotton bags, wooden boxes (or shelves) and clay dishes are all great options. Try to avoid keeping your crystals in plastic bags or containers for any length of time, as this may begin to sap their energy.

If you are transporting your crystals, a great tip for protecting your more fragile pieces is to cover delicate crystal points and edges with a ball of Blu Tack (or other similar gently adhesive substance). Not only does this safeguard the tip from chipping and breaking, but it also creates an energetic 'block' or barrier for the stream of energy coming from the crystal point.

ATTUNING TO YOUR CRYSTALS

When you acquire a new crystal for healing purposes, it is important to connect with it energetically. This is called 'attuning' to the crystal. Different methods of attuning to your new crystal can include meditating with it, sleeping with it under your pillow and carrying it around with you. The more closely you attune to your crystal, the more powerful the healing work will be.

THE PHYSICS AND METAPHYSICS OF CRYSTAL HEALING

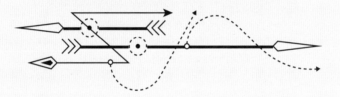

FANTASTIC FOUR — CRYSTAL HEALING'S FOUR ENERGETIC PRINCIPLES

In crystal healing, it is acknowledged that all crystals and stones are unique, both in appearance and in energy. A crystal is selected for healing based on its colour, energy and metaphysical associations. Taking this into consideration, crystal healing works energetically with four main principles: vibration, colour, chakras and chi (or life energy).

UNIVERSAL LAW OF VIBRATION

It is generally accepted among experts of science and philosophy that the fabric of our existence is governed by a set of universal laws. This book is not aiming to unlock the mysteries of the universe (so I won't be exploring these now); however, there is one law that is essential to understand when working with crystals or any other form of energetic healing. This is the law of vibration.

The law of vibration states that nothing in the universe is ever perfectly still. Everything that exists in the universe (whether seen or unseen) is made up of vibrational frequency and moving particles. With help from advanced microscopes we have determined that even seemingly solid objects (such as furniture, people or rocks) are made up of constantly moving and vibrating molecules, atoms, sub-atomic particles and quanta (the smallest measurable particles).

More interesting is the fact that if we look more closely at an atom we see that it is actually mostly made up of empty space with vibrating parts within it. We know that most atoms contain a nucleus as well as neutrons, positively charged protons and negatively charged electrons. But these are tiny in comparison to the size of the atom as a whole. Somehow, through this cloud of empty atomic space, these sub-atomic particles are able to constantly interact and communicate with each other electromagnetically.

This means that, in the physical world, what our eyes perceive as a solid object is really just a constantly vibrating mass of atoms that are largely made up of empty space, through which electromagnetic energy can travel.

You might be wondering how this relates to crystal healing.

If everything in the entire physical universe is simply clumps of electrically charged, vibrating particles floating in space, then it stands to reason that something about the nature of this empty space is a perfect conduit for energy. After all, how can the electrons, protons and neutronsall communicate with each other if their energy wasn't somehow connected through the atomic space? Further to this, each atom communicates energetically with its neighbouring atoms, which, when multiplied by the millions, make up a whole physical object, like a tree or a person.

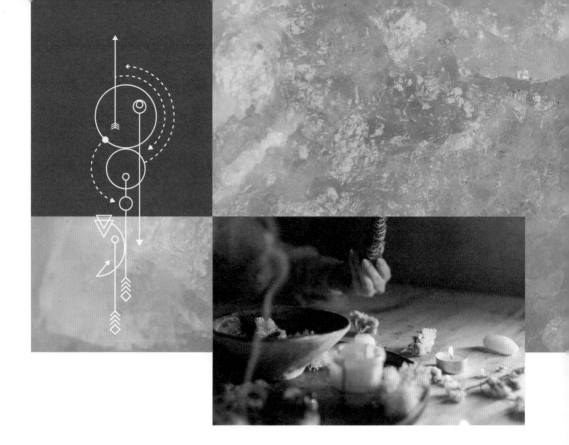

The very nature of the universe is vibrational and energetic. Nothing is still and nothing remains unchanged – from the electrons and protons spinning around inside an atom to the neurons firing in your brain as you read this. Energy, in its purest life-form, is contained within every single cell of your being. How else does a single egg cell and single sperm cell join and, without any conscious thought or direction, multiply each day to grow arms, legs, a brain and eventually a fully realised consciousness?

We are getting into the realm of quantum science now, as we do not yet have the tools or knowledge to understand how the micro-universe works, so anything here on in is purely theoretical, but it poses the question:

If space is the perfect conduit for carrying and transferring energy between molecules inside a single atom and between atoms, then, by the same logic, shouldn't it be able to transfer energy *between physical objects and their surrounding environment* because everything is made up of the exact same stuff?

If this is the case (and I believe it is), then vibrational energy connects every living being and object in existence.

When we work with crystals on a human being, we harness the energy from within the crystal and transfer it to the person, using space as the conduit. The crystal can also receive energy from the person in the same way and can therefore absorb pain, trauma and negative vibrational energy from the person being treated.

COLOUR THERAPY

It can be difficult to understand why many crystals are assigned specific healing properties – because who decides these things anyway? Often, the physical appearance of a crystal will give a clue as to its vibrational healing properties.

Clear Quartz, for example, is a beautifully clear and transparent stone, and is therefore excellent for channelling clarity. Rose Quartz, on the other hand, is a soft, pale pink colour. Most crystal lovers would be familiar with its reputation for being a stone of love and for opening the Heart Chakra. This is because its soft colour and energetic vibration resonate with the human experience of emotion.

If we look at pale pink from a colour therapy perspective, it is easy to understand why this colour is also often associated with baby girls and femininity, because pale pink, as an energy, is soft, gentle, feminine and loving.

Now consider the energy of deep red or orange. Imagine yourself surrounded by red or orange and observe the change in

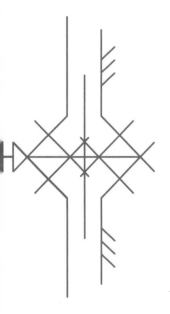

your energetic state. Warm, bright colours are much more stimulating than pale pink and might awaken feelings of action, energy, strength, creativity, power or intensity. Similarly, we can use red and orange crystals on the lower chakras to bring vitality, energy, stamina and cleansing to someone who is feeling lethargic or 'flat'.

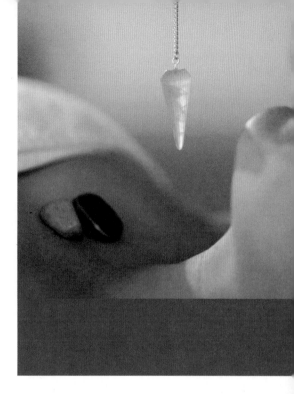

CHAKRAS

According to ancient Yogic philosophy, the human body (and its energy field) contains areas of concentrated energy called chakras. Each chakra on the body vibrates with its own unique colour resonance and has its own body association and meaning. By placing matching coloured crystals directly on the chakras, we can tap in to the person's energy much more accurately than by placing the stone randomly on the body.

For example, the Throat Chakra (which radiates out from the cervical spine, but can be best sensed at the dip of the throat) is represented by the colour blue. It is associated with communication, expression and thyroid health. Therefore, a crystal therapist will usually work with blue crystals directly over this chakra for throat and communication issues. We will further explore the chakras and their energetic associations in the following chapters (see page 59).

CHI — LIFE-FORCE ENERGY

The Chinese concept of Chi, or life-force energy (sometimes spelled as Qi), stems from the law of vibration and is applied through energetic healing. It explains how all areas of our physical body are linked through energetic channels known as meridians and teaches us how we can work with the meridians to balance energy within the body.

It is important to have a good understanding of how energy flows throughout the body so we can use crystals with more effect during a healing session. For example, most people know that we feel emotional trauma through the Heart Chakra, but don't realise that trauma, like all energetically 'heavy' energy, flows down the body and often gets stuck around the digestive and lower back areas (around the Sacral Chakra). So, it would be much more effective for the crystal work to be focused on the lower body, instead of the heart area.

PEE-AY-ZO-WHAT? THE SCIENCE OF CRYSTAL HEALING

While there may be some disharmony between physicists and metaphysicians regarding the inner workings of the universe, what can be agreed upon is that both physics and metaphysics have their roots firmly grounded in the concept of energy. Physics deals primarily with energy that can be measured, quantified and understood, whereas metaphysics focuses more on energy that we are yet to conventionally understand or control.

Rocks have a basic energetic vibration called a 'resonant frequency', which is the measurable oscillation of the stone in its natural, at-rest state. A crystal's resonant frequency will depend on its unique molecular structure and mineral composition. This frequency is measured in units called hertz (Hz). Quartz crystal, for example, has an at-rest resonant frequency that never varies, meaning it vibrates at a constant and precise rate.

What will impress the pants off any sceptic is the fact that Quartz crystal can influence, change and respond to different mechanical and energetic forces around it, because it is uniquely *piezoelectric* (pronounced *pee-ay-zo-electric*). 'Piezoelectricity' refers to a measurable energetic charge that develops inside a solid substance in response to mechanical stimulation. It can also absorb magnetic and electric energy from its environment and convert this to mechanical energy (or movement).

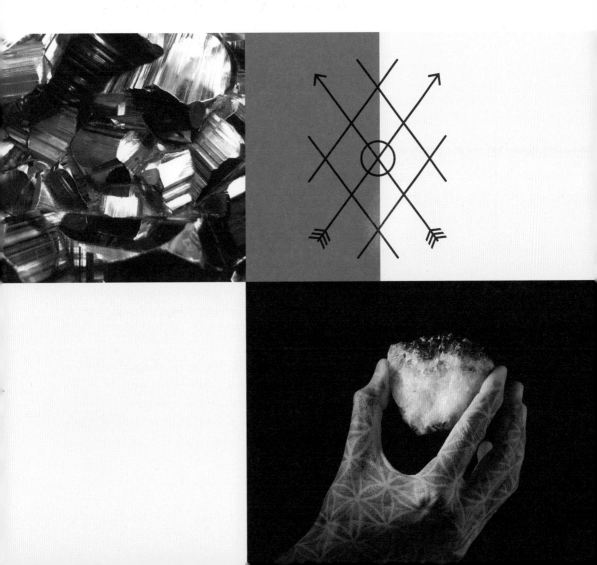

This exciting discovery was made by a couple of French brothers named Jacques and Pierre Curie in 1880. (If these names sound familiar, it is because Pierre Curie was the husband of the Nobel Prize–winning scientist Marie Curie.) The young Curie brothers observed that certain minerals responded mechanically when exposed to magnetic fields and named this phenomenon piezoelectricity. To further their work, they created the Piezoelectric Quartz Electrometer. It was the starting point for what was later developed into the truly life-changing technology that underpins almost all digital electronic circuits. Most people would be astounded to discover that nearly all modern computer technology (such as smart phones, LCD screens and microchips) would not be possible without harnessing the energetic properties of the humble Quartz crystal.

Let me explain.

Most rocks contain a chemical compound called silicon dioxide in various quantities. Silicon dioxide, when paired with the unique cellular structure of certain crystals, is like a recipe for energetic alchemy. Quartz crystal contains just the right amount of silicon dioxide and has just the right cellular structure to form a crystal that is piezoelectric. There are only a few other substances on Earth (such as bones and DNA) that are considered piezoelectric.

This means when a Quartz crystal is mechanically stimulated (through touch, for example), it can generate an electrical charge within itself. It does this by transforming the mechanical energy from the friction of the touch into another form (electricity). When you squeeze a Quartz crystal, it generates a tiny, measurable electric current. Some other crystals have this ability too.

In the simplest terms, piezoelectric technology uses crystals to convert mechanical energy into electricity.

This principle also works in reverse. If you pass electricity through Quartz, it vibrates at a precise frequency (it shakes an exact number of times) each second. People sensitive to energy can even feel this subtle pulse with their bare hands!

In fact, piezoelectric crystals have been instrumental in shifting humanity from the industrial age to the age of digital technology. Some might consider this one of the most important evolutionary leaps in the consciousness of humanity.

Two modern technologies that would not exist without piezoelectric crystals are sonar and clocks. Sonar technology was used for detecting ultrasonic submarines in the First World War. This was the first known application of piezoelectricity in documented history and was made possible by sticking quartz crystals between two steel plates with a hydrophone (underwater detection device) attached.

Have you ever wondered what makes the hand of a clock or watch tick? Inside an analogue clock or watch, the battery sends electricity to a tiny Quartz crystal through an electronic circuit. The Quartz crystal absorbs this electrical current and outputs it as

mechanical energy. The crystal oscillates (vibrates back and forth) at a precise frequency, which is exactly 32,768 times each second. The circuit counts the number of vibrations and uses them to generate regular electric pulses, which amounts to one per second, giving us a 'tick' every second. (This is the reason why one of the most well-known watch brands in the world is named Quartz!)

I won't go into a scientific explanation for every piece of modern technology that relies on piezoelectric crystals (I encourage you to do your own research), but here are a few more everyday items that would not be possible without piezoelectric crystals:

◊   lighters
◊   camera lenses
◊   microphones
◊   microchips
◊   ultrasound machines
◊   inkjet printers
◊   record players
◊   LCD (Liquid Crystal Display) screens.

HUMAN, MEET ROCK — CRYSTALS IN THE HUMAN ENERGY FIELD

Unlike crystals, human beings are energetically volatile and complex. Each cell in our body can produce enormous amounts of energy in the form of heat and electrical pulses (think about kinetic energy and all the electrical impulses firing from our neurons).

When working with our own energy, we need to understand that our vibrational state can change in seconds. Factors such as environment, health and social situations play a large role in how we maintain our energetic state. The very nature of the extended human energy field (the aura) is to expand out beyond the physical skin barrier and mingle with the energy of the surrounding environment and people.

Take a minute to imagine how you would feel standing in a beautiful garden. You might feel calm, peaceful, connected or inspired. Now think about how you would feel walking across a busy intersection in a big city. You might feel stressed, excited, rushed or confused. These different feelings permeate your entire energetic being. This affects your energy and causes your vibrational state to respond and change.

Just as your environment can profoundly affect your energetic state, a crystal can also influence your energy when it is placed in close contact with you.

We already know that crystals can absorb and transmute electrical and mechanical energy, and a human being generates vast amounts of energy. The real magic happens when the two are brought together and 'talk' to one another through energetic channels. The crystal can absorb energy from the human body, transmute and transform it, and return it back into the body — cleansed, reprogrammed and recharged.

APATITE OR APPETITE — UNDERSTANDING ENERGETIC TRAUMA

The human 'body' is so much more than a single, physical entity made of flesh and bone. Since any form of trauma affects the human body energetically, we need to understand how, by looking at the energetic system multi-dimensionally.

The human energy system is a complete functioning whole, made up of individual but interconnected parts. I call these parts the energetic bodies and they include the physical body, the emotional body, the psychological body, the spiritual body and the ego body. You might even consider these as different aspects of Self.

There is a close relationship between the different energetic bodies and the chakra system. For example, the Heart Chakra is the gateway to the emotional body and the Root Chakra is the gateway to the physical body.

Here is a summary of the different energetic bodies that make up the human energy system:

◊   The **physical body** is the part of us that exists entirely in the physical world as flesh and bone.

◊   The **emotional body** is the part of us that encompasses our emotional world. It is a place of feeling, loving and emotional experience.

◊   The **psychological body** is the part of us responsible for our thought patterns, programming, belief systems and mental wellness.

◊   The **spiritual body** is our Highest Self. It is the part of us that is connected to everything that ever was and will be, through universal consciousness. The spiritual body presents itself through inspiration, joy, intuition, purpose, resonance and true wisdom.

◊ The **ego body** is the shadow of our spiritual body. Just like light cannot exist without shadow, these two bodies are eternally bound together. The ego body is the part of us that is unique and expressed as an individual (distinct from the collective universal consciousness), through our personal identity.

Imbalance or blockage in the energy system can usually be felt through a specific chakra and will reveal itself through a set of recognisable symptoms, from physical illness to behavioural patterns and even psychological disorders.

Any pain, grief, challenge, injury or adversity we experience can cause energetic trauma to one or more of our energetic bodies. For example, a broken bone will cause energetic trauma to the physical body and heartbreak will energetically traumatise the emotional

body. This trauma can ripple throughout our entire energy system and may manifest symptomatically in any part of our energetic body. Here are some examples of how energetic trauma can manifest symptomatically in different areas of the energetic body:

> **Example 1** – A person feeling mental pressure and stress at work begins to experience painful migraines. This is a physical manifestation (headache pain) of a psychological trauma (stress). In other words, a trauma experienced through the psychological body has manifested symptomatically in the physical body.

> **Example 2** – A person has been the victim of emotional abuse and later develops an eating disorder, leading to obesity. This is a physical manifestation (obesity) of an emotional trauma (emotional abuse). In other words, a trauma experienced through the emotional body has manifested symptomatically in the physical body through emotional overeating.

When working energetically with crystals, we must try to understand the *true* nature and cause of the trauma before we can select the best possible crystals for the healing. To do this, we should explore how the symptoms are connected to a root trauma, rather than focusing exclusively on the presenting symptoms.

Most mainstream crystal healing takes the one-dimensional approach to treatment. In the case of the overweight person mentioned in Example 2 above, this would involve selecting crystals that correlate directly with the client's symptom of being overweight or overeating. An appropriate choice might be Apatite, which is an ironically named crystal, popular for weight loss. I call this the 'describe and prescribe' approach, in which a person describes their symptoms and the crystal therapist prescribes the 'quick fix' crystal for those symptoms. This is not a Spiritual Rebel's approach!

To achieve more transformational and lasting healing results, a Spiritual Rebel needs to journey deeper, beyond the usual 'X crystal is good for Y result' approach.

A more multi-dimensional approach is to first get to the root cause of the symptoms. What I mean by this is delving more deeply into the reasons *why* the person is in their current physical state, rather than focusing only on the presenting symptoms themselves. Many (but not all) cases of obesity and overeating are caused by an underlying feeling of self-loathing or worthlessness, usually resulting from a history of emotionally traumatic experiences.

So, if we were working with the overweight person mentioned in Example 2, then it would be worthwhile exploring whether or not the person has a history of emotionally or psychologically damaging relationships, abandonment in childhood, bullying, failure and so on.

If so, then instead of focusing our crystal work on suppressing appetite or encouraging weight loss, we should be focusing on strengthening the person's sense of self-worth, self-acceptance and 'belonging' in the world, as well as healing the past.

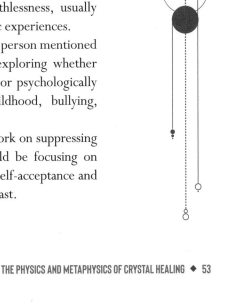

At the Heart and Solar Plexus chakras, we should use crystals that offer support, acceptance, love, confidence, health and vitality on the emotional, physical and spiritual levels. By working on the Sacral and Root chakras too, we can encourage the release of trauma trapped in the gut, while energetically cleansing and detoxifying the digestive organs.

Beneficial stones for this specific case might include:

Citrine – for self-confidence, overcoming addiction (food), inspiration, positivity, and cleansing and releasing old patterning relating to self-loathing.

Rhodonite and Rose Quartz – to heal and softly open the Heart Chakra to welcome and receive deep, fulfilling self-love. Also, to gently release emotional trauma stuck in the emotional body.

Orthoceras – for providing a time-link back into childhood (and beyond) to help bring acceptance and reconciliation of past events. Also, to provide firm grounding for a person whose formative years were decidedly ungrounded.

Whether you are navigating your own healing journey or working with a partner or client, it is important to approach each step with unconditional love and without judgement. Judgement has *no* place in the healing journey (see next page). Our goal should always be to remain open, accepting and perceptive without being presumptuous.

To give you more of an understanding of how trauma can manifest in the energetic body, here are examples of some of the most common manifestations I have encountered during my years as a professional crystal therapist:

◊ emotional trauma, manifesting in the gut as digestive issues, food intolerances, allergies, weight gain and bloating

◊ emotional baggage, manifesting in the spine as chronic or degenerative back pain (unrelated to injury), or as tightness and tension in the shoulders (from lugging around all that additional energetic weight!)

◊ stress and overthinking, manifesting in the head as headaches and tension

◊ oppression or stifling of personal expression, manifesting in the throat as varying throat disorders, neck pain and shoulder tension.

When considering how trauma manifests in the body, we must be realistic about what level of healing we can achieve using crystal therapy alone.

It is not realistic to expect that, by placing a single type of crystal on your body, all your pain and trauma will magically disappear. Healing is not a passive experience. You need to be active in your own healing journey and take ownership of your healing outcomes. If you have acute lower back pain because you tried to

HEALING JOURNEY

The path to healing is not a clean, linear transition from a beginning point to a finite end point. Most spiritual philosophies regard the healing path as a journey rich with emotion, self-discovery and realisation. In transpersonal circles, the healing journey is sometimes referred to as the 'hero's journey', which draws parallels between the healing path and a mythological hero's brave journey of triumph over adversity.

lift a heavy couch, then it is highly unlikely that placing a crystal on your lower back is going to miraculously 'cure' your injury! Yes, there are crystals that can be effective in relieving pain and inflammation in the body, but, just like any other healing treatment (clinical, energetic, medical or otherwise), there should never be an expectation that the treatment is the stand-alone answer.

I am regularly contacted by people all over the world asking which crystal would best help them with a specific symptom or situation. Yet without knowing their personal history or understanding their complex and unique energetic state, it is impossible to offer specific personalised advice.

By passing complete ownership of your healing to any outside source (such as a pill, a crystal or a practitioner), you are completely disempowering yourself and limiting your own amazing healing potential. Crystals work with your energetic vibration. If you are positive and genuinely willing to do the work and help yourself, then your healing outcome will be much more effective than that of a person who is completely disempowered and approaches their healing with scepticism, passivity or defeat.

CRYSTAL HEALING AND THE CHAKRAS

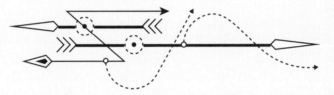

WHEELS, COLOURS AND CONES — INTRODUCING NINE CHAKRAS

To gain a deeper understanding of how crystal healing works with the human energy system, we need to understand how our energy system functions within our body.

The word 'chakra' comes from the ancient Indian Sanskrit language and literally means 'wheel'. Throughout many Eastern wellness practices (such as yoga and pranic energy healing), it is accepted that the human body holds certain high-vibrational energy points. These energy centres exist as spinning wheels of prana (life-force energy).

The body's main chakras are connected to the spine and radiate out through the energetic body (or aura) as spinning 'cones' of energy. These chakras spin continuously,

funnelling energy throughout the body and energy field and can be felt at specific points on and outside the body.

The human body is a complex energy system comprising hundreds of minor and major chakras. You are likely already familiar with the seven main chakras made popular by yoga and modern wellness practices; however, in this book you will learn to work with nine.

Ancient knowledge teaches us that each chakra has a specific name, body location and colour association. Each chakra is represented by a unique colour, because of the way individual chakras can be experienced visually and energetically through colour vibration. Chakras can also be experienced through other senses, including touch, taste and sound vibration.

Here is an overview of the nine chakras featured in this book with their sensory location on the body (where you can feel them) and their colour associations.

EARTH CHAKRA (OR EARTH STAR CHAKRA)
Location: approximately 15 centimetres (6 inches) below the feet
Colour: dark brown

ROOT CHAKRA (OR BASE CHAKRA)

Location: at the perineum, between the anus and genitals

Colour: red

SACRAL CHAKRA

Location: just below the navel

Colour: orange

SOLAR PLEXUS CHAKRA

Location: between the navel and heart, at the base of ribs

Colour: yellow

HEART CHAKRA

Location: centre of chest, over the heart (see next page)

Colour: green (sometimes pink)

THROAT CHAKRA

Location: in the 'hollow' of the throat

Colour: blue

THIRD EYE CHAKRA

Location: between the eyebrows (or just above)

Colour: indigo

CROWN CHAKRA

Location: centre top of head/forehead

Colour: violet

HIGHER CROWN (OR SOUL STAR CHAKRA)

Location: approximately 15 centimetres (6 inches) above the top of the head

Colour: white

Just above the Heart Chakra, between the heart and the throat, is the Higher Heart Chakra. It is so closely related to the Heart Chakra that it is often not included in chakra diagrams. For most crystal healing sessions, it is fine to simply address the Heart Chakra and leave out the Higher Heart. However, I do work specifically with the Higher Heart Chakra in some of the body layouts in Part 3, when the layout requires extra attention on emotional healing.

LEARN TO SPEAK CHAKRA — UNDERSTANDING CHAKRA ENERGY

Some highly attuned people can see the chakras in all their glorious colours. Others can feel a chakra by receiving and interpreting energetic signals such as sound, temperature, air density, taste or vibrational quivers. Perhaps you are already highly attuned and can sense or see the chakras. However, if you are at the start of your spiritual journey, these skills can be learned with focus and practice.

Everyone experiences energy differently. As I mentioned earlier, my first experience with crystals was an intensely visual one, with flashing lights and colours, but also changes in temperature. The first time I had a full set of chakra crystals placed on my body, a whole new world of swirling colours and imagery was revealed to me. I also went from cold to feeling incredibly hot, as my own energy was amplified by the energy of the crystals. (To this day, I always wear a sleeveless shirt whenever I am working with crystals or facilitating a crystal workshop, because I still get insanely hot!)

If you are new to crystal healing, a great way to start developing your sensory ability is to practise feeling your own energy. Try this exercise as a starting point.

ACTIVITY: FEEL YOUR OWN CHAKRA ENERGY

Begin by getting into a comfortable position and taking some slow, deep breaths. Focus on clearing your mind of thoughts and distractions until you are in a state of heightened awareness and mindful presence.

When you are completely present, gently position one of your hands a few inches in front of your face, with your palm facing towards you.

Sweep your hand very slowly down the centre of your body, keeping about 5–10 centimetres (2–4 inches) away from your skin. Focus all your attention into your hand and fingertips, noticing any sensations you might begin to feel. You might even like to try this with a Clear Quartz point, holding the point towards you. You may feel one or more of the following sensations.

HEAT

Heat is the easiest and most common energetic sensation to feel. The human body produces a large amount of heat energy, so this can be an excellent starting point for determining whether a chakra is moving freely or is blocked.

Gentle pleasant warmth usually indicates that a chakra is flowing and active. 'Prickly hot' heat is more often associated with blockage and inflammation in the energetic body.

COLD

Feeling cold throughout the energetic body may range from a pleasant coolness to an 'empty' or 'icy' coldness.

Refreshing coolness in a chakra might indicate openness, clarity or a recent cleansing. An unwelcome coldness could point to defensiveness, denial or closure of the chakra (such as a closed Heart Chakra for emotional protection).

TINGLING

A pleasant tingling sensation usually indicates that a chakra is active and in reasonable health.

Intense tingling might suggest that there is an expansion or opening occurring in that chakra and that the energy is strong. It is common to feel warmth and tingling through the Third Eye Chakra of a person who is experiencing a period of spiritual awakening, for example.

DRAGGING

If you feel as though your hand is 'stuck' or 'dragging' through a chakra, then this is a clear indication of unresolved energetic trauma and blockage in the area.

Energy flows through the body like a river. If too much debris or rubbish is dumped into the river's flow, then the river will eventually become blocked. The water will build up pressure on one side of the blockage and will be reduced to a small trickle on the other side. This is exactly what happens to the flow of energy in your body when there is a large blockage. The energy flow becomes stuck.

Energy that can't flow freely can negatively affect your health and may even prevent you from 'moving forward' with aspects of your life (also known as feeling stuck in a rut).

PULLING

Sometimes, you may feel your hand being pulled to one side of a chakra or being pushed away, rather than moving through the chakra space. This can indicate imbalance, subconscious defensiveness, protection mechanisms, avoidance or deviation from one's true path.

The energetic body sets up this response as a protective measure, to prevent a perceived trauma from entering the chakra. In my experience, it is most common to experience this type of response at the Heart and Throat chakras, which are most closely related to the emotions.

VIBRATION

Vibrational sensations may vary from a slight quivering to uncontrollable shaking. This feeling could indicate active energy flowing or a profound awakening or ascension process occurring.

Please keep in mind that these sensory descriptions are examples only and are not to be used as a definitive diagnostic tool. To best understand chakra energy, it is essential to also consider the emotional and intuitive *feeling* that accompanies the energetic sensations you have detected.

Every person is different: one person may perceive heat as a positive indication, while, for another, this may indicate imbalance or illness. Remember, there is no 'one size fits all' when it comes to energetic healing, so it is important to maintain an open mind.

The first step to working successfully with energy (and honouring your inner Spiritual Rebel) is to understand how *you* sense and process the world around you. Think about times when you may have experienced unexplained chills, surges of emotion or the feeling that someone is invading your personal space. These are all energetic responses to external energy forces.

Just like learning a spoken language, the key to mastering the language of energy is to practise as much as possible. The more you practise working with energy, the more accurate you will become in interpreting vibrational messages.

By regularly observing your own responses to energetic stimuli, you will soon be able to understand how energy 'speaks' to you.

WHAT TO LOOK FOR — SYMPTOMS OF CHAKRA IMBALANCE

Diagnosing imbalance and blockage in the energetic body is not dissimilar to diagnosing imbalance or illness in the physical body.

There is usually a range of common symptoms to look for, which will give the practitioner a better idea of what the root illness or injury is. For example, if you fall and twist your ankle, there are some key symptoms that you or your medical practitioner would look for to better understand your injury, such as swelling, limited range of movement and discolouration.

Similarly, trauma experienced by any part of the energetic body will manifest in a variety of commonly presented symptoms. These might be physical, behavioural, emotional, psychological or spiritual. Recognising and understanding these symptoms is the first step towards deciphering what your (or your partner's) body is telling you. This will result in much more targeted and effective crystal healing treatment.

Before we delve further into understanding the language of the chakras and the energy system, please keep in mind that every person is different. There are many factors that contribute to ill health and *all* factors should be considered when drawing diagnostic conclusions about yourself or those around you.

The following information explains how each chakra relates to a specific body region or area of wellness, and what symptoms may be present to indicate blockage or imbalance in that energy centre.

HIGHER CROWN AND CROWN CHAKRAS

Because the Higher Crown and Crown chakras are so closely related, the physical associations and symptoms are almost identical. Therefore, these chakras can be combined for the following interpretations.

Physical associations

These chakras pertain to spirit, creation, connectedness, life purpose, Higher Self and the brain and nervous system. The Higher Crown is often represented in ancient artwork as a white glow or halo around the head of enlightened individuals, such as Jesus and Buddha. This symbolises a fully awakened Higher Crown Chakra and connection to spirit.

Possible symptoms

Headaches, depression, feeling 'lost' or confused about your direction, addictions, psychological disorders, nervous disorders, having no spiritual belief, feeling like the world is against you, and lack of compassion, empathy or remorse.

THIRD EYE CHAKRA

Physical associations

This chakra is the centre of our psychic power. It relates to awareness, clairvoyance, intuition, inner wisdom and the forehead and temples.

Possible symptoms

Tension pain or headaches in the forehead, blurry vision, inability to focus, feeling disconnected and uninspired, feeling untrusting and sceptical, being unable to accept or learn from life's challenges or to learn from mistakes, being stuck in the same patterns, fear of change and wilful stubbornness.

THROAT CHAKRA

Physical associations

This chakra is connected to expression, communication, expressing your own 'soul language', giving and receiving, truth seeking, personal integrity, arms, legs, throat, mouth and ears.

Possible symptoms

Sore or croaky throat, cough, difficulty swallowing or tasting, neck pain, shoulder pain, inner ear and throat disorders, thyroid issues, loss of desire to express yourself, lying or exaggerating, lack of confidence speaking and loss of soul language (see page 72).

HEART CHAKRA

Physical associations

The Heart Chakra is the home of the emotional self. It is the centre for love, kindness, compassion, acceptance and forgiveness, and it relates to the blood, lungs, circulatory system, upper chest and immune system.

Possible symptoms

Heartburn, tender chest or chest tightness, shallow breathing, sleep apnoea, inability to trust, emotionally defensive, commitment issues in relationships, emotionally 'cold' or unstable (such as crying a lot), lack of compassion, fear of being emotionally hurt, self-loathing or judgement, always putting others first (which can be symbolic of both a kind heart and self-love avoidance), feeling generally imbalanced and feeling emotionally disconnected.

SOLAR PLEXUS CHAKRA

Physical associations

This chakra is closely related to the Heart Chakra in some ways. It connects specifically with Ego, sense of Self, success, motivation, inspiration, self-esteem, empowerment, control, emotional burden, upper digestion, muscles, skin and eyes.

Possible symptoms

Self-loathing, helplessness, low self-esteem, lack of motivation, lethargy, over-dependence on others, lack of initiative, lack of courage, fear of being judged or rejected, prioritising the happiness of others, feeling stuck in a rut, avoiding change because it is 'too hard', overeating, weight issues, unhealthy lifestyle habits, upper digestive issues (such as indigestion and burping), complaining about life but not initiating change, having a 'Why me?' mentality and depression.

SACRAL CHAKRA

Physical associations

This chakra relates to the Ego and the physical, more 'human' experiences of desire, creativity and pleasure, reproductive organs, sexuality, energy levels, physical health and lumbar spine.

Possible symptoms

Low libido, lower digestive issues (such as nausea and bloating), weight gain through the mid-section, food cravings, lack of motivation, lack of excitement or passion, unhealthy desires (such as addictions), low energy, low stamina, feeling lethargic, lower back pain, infertility and reproductive health issues, erectile dysfunction (men), inability to orgasm (women), self-denial and being prone to physical sickness.

ROOT CHAKRA

Physical associations

This chakra is the seat of physical power and represents attachment to the physical world. It is connected to your incarnation on this earthly plane, instinct, lower body, survival, kundalini, grounding, the nose and organs of elimination.

Possible symptoms

Feeling ungrounded, feeling unsure of your path, feeling lost, lower back pain, infertility and reproductive health issues, erectile dysfunction (men), inability to orgasm (women), lower digestive issues (such as constipation or diarrhoea), feeling disconnected from family, heavy and painful periods (women), and feeling like you are just 'getting by'.

EARTH CHAKRA

Physical associations

This chakra is for grounding, connecting with the Earth and your ancestral line, human history, foundations and the feet.

Possible symptoms

Feeling ungrounded, disconnected from your family, 'flighty', jumping from job to job or idea to idea without 'landing', personal identity crisis, very high arches in feet, pain in ankles or feet, chaotic or disorganised life, family 'issues' (especially with parents), and feeling unstable or uncomfortable being barefoot.

Once we understand the role each chakra plays within our energy system and how imbalance can manifest symptomatically in the body, we can approach our healing with much more clarity and effect.

Remember, energy is both universal and unique. No two people will ever have the same energetic imprint. You may relate to all the symptoms outlined above for a specific chakra or you may relate to none. Therefore, it is important to use your intuition as a navigational tool and listen to what your Higher Self is telling you.

SOUL LANGUAGE

'Soul language' is a term I use to describe the way in which you communicate and express your deepest, most authentic Self with the world. This is completely different from your day-to-day spoken communication. How do you express your innermost feelings and your pure spirit 'essence' with the world? Is it through music, art, poetry, designing, building, gardening, drawing, singing or something else? This form of pure, joyful expression is your soul language.

PART

2

A REBEL'S GUIDE TO PRACTICAL CRYSTAL HEALING

CRUISING THE ENERGY HIGHWAY — WORKING WITH NATURAL ENERGY FLOW

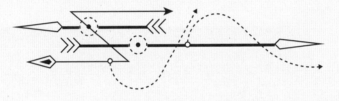

Earlier, I mentioned that the flow of energy runs through our bodies like a river. An even more powerful metaphor might be to think of the energy flow as a two-lane highway that runs the entire length of your body. Just as a regular highway has two directions of traffic (or movement), so does the energy that flows through your energy highway. Energy is constantly flowing in through your Higher Crown Chakra, travelling down your body and exiting through the Root Chakra and Earth Chakra. It also constantly flows in through the Earth Chakra, up the length of your body and out through your Higher Crown Chakra in a never-ending loop of energy.

To achieve optimum health and wellness, it is vital that both sides of the highway stay clear to prevent 'traffic' from building up and causing a significant energetic obstruction on one or both sides. To keep both sides clear, we can work with the natural direction of the energy flow to remove energetic blockage and keep the traffic flowing freely.

Physical toxins and waste products are removed from the body through the organs of elimination at the Root Chakra. Energetic waste is also eliminated through this energy centre. Blockage caused by pain and trauma is energetically heavy, so over time it naturally migrates *down* the body. Once there, it may be released through the Root Chakra, but it can get stuck somewhere along the way (commonly around the Sacral Chakra, where we process not only food, but energy too).

Once we understand this, we can use the *downflow* of energy to help unblock the chakras, remove energetic trauma and cleanse the energy system. One way of working harmoniously with the downflow of energy for cleansing is to create a crystal layout on the lower chakras. The crystals act like a magnet and pull blocked energy *downwards* and out of the body. Crystals that help with cleansing and grounding include Hematite, Red Jasper, Carnelian and Bloodstone.

Energies such as inspiration, joy and love are very light and uplifting, so they naturally flow *upwards* through the body to connect with the Higher Crown Chakra. Therefore, any work that focuses on stimulating and raising energetic vibration should move with the *upflow* of energy in the body. We can do this by creating a high-vibe crystal layout on the higher chakras, which will attract the energies *upwards*. Crystals that help to raise the vibration and energise the chakras include Clear Quartz, Purple Fluorite, Amethyst, Celestite, Selenite and Clear Calcite.

WAND WAVING — USING CRYSTAL WANDS

As mentioned previously, crystal wands are used dynamically in a healing session to direct energy around the body and perform more complex crystal healing techniques, such as cleansing and charging the chakras and drawing pain out of the body.

A good quality, crystal healing wand forms the basis of your crystal healing practice, so it is worth investing in a piece that you truly resonate with. I prefer using a large, natural Lemurian Laser Quartz wand.

Before performing any wand work, make sure you are holding your wand comfortably in your hand. It is important to grip it loosely, so that the sensitive nerve endings in your fingertips are not squashed (because you'll need these to detect subtle vibrations

in the wand). While your hold on the wand should be gentle, it needs to be secure enough that there is no risk of dropping the wand unexpectedly. The last thing you want is for your partner to be deep in a relaxing meditation then suddenly find the pointy end of a crystal wand in their eye!

When moving the wand, try to keep your movements smooth and flowing. Remember that energy itself is always in a constant state of flow and movement. Jerky, clumsy wand movements do little to create energetic harmony.

Start by relaxing and loosening your wrists and arms. Practise holding your wand comfortably out in front of you and focus your attention on the energy flowing through your arms and fingers into the wand. Think of the wand as an extension of yourself, rather than a separate object.

You can take this activity further by rolling your wrist around to 'draw' circles in the air with your wand. Focus on creating smooth movements and let your body just move in flow with the energy. Once your wand feels comfortable and your arm is loose, you are ready to start the crystal work.

CHANNEL PAIN OR BLOCKAGE AWAY FROM SPECIFIC AREAS

To draw out pain or energy from a specific part of the body (such as localised headache pain), gently press the blunt end of a single-terminated wand against your (or your partner's) body. Make sure that the blunt end is in contact with the body and the point of the wand is facing outwards.

Hold the wand in place for several minutes and visualise the unwanted energy (or pain) being siphoned out of the body by the wand, which it releases through its laser-like tip.

CHANNEL HEALING ENERGY INTO A SPECIFIC AREA

To channel a stream of healing energy into a specific area (such as into the ovaries to stimulate ovulation or into the Solar Plexus Chakra to promote self-acceptance), press the pointed tip of a single-terminated crystal wand gently against the area to be treated.

Hold the wand here for several minutes, while also visualising white or gold healing energy flowing through the wand and into the treatment area.

This technique works in reverse to the previous technique, which was drawing blockages away. Here, the outward-facing blunt end of the wand captures and draws in universal light energy, while the pointed end amplifies and delivers it into the body.

ALIGN THE CHAKRAS

This is a simple technique you can use almost anywhere. When you are feeling a little imbalanced, this quick wand alignment can work wonders!

Hold a single-terminated wand in front of your (or your partner's) forehead with the tip pointed towards the top of the head, at the Crown Chakra.

If working on a partner, slowly and steadily move the wand down the centre line of their body, which is the main meridian through which the most powerful chakras sit. Be sure to keep the wand tip pointed towards their body and try not to stop or move the wand around too much. The goal is to remain as steady as possible. Keep moving the wand smoothly, in one straight line, until you reach their feet, or Earth Chakra. Once you have reached this point, move the wand back up the main meridian again.

If you are performing this alignment on yourself, try to keep your body straight as you move your wand down the centre of your body, until you reach your groin, or Root Chakra. Once you've reached this chakra, move the wand back up again.

By moving the wand in a downwards direction, you encourage cleansing and grounding through the lower chakras. Upwards motion encourages connection to the Higher Self and stimulates energy flow throughout the body.

The up and down wand movement can be repeated as many times as it takes for you to begin feeling more centred and aligned.

This technique is so fast and simple that it can be performed in a quick 5-minute break at work or in between tasks on a busy day.

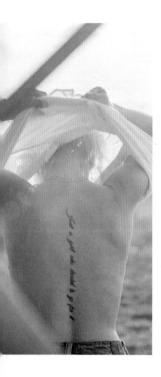

If you prefer working with a pendulum, then feel free to modify the above techniques to suit your needs. I suggest lying down (face up) and holding the pendulum a couple of inches above the body. Move between the Crown Chakra and Earth Chakra if working on a partner, or the Crown Chakra and Root Chakra if working on yourself. Be prepared: the pendulum might swing wildly over chakras that are out of balance or alignment.

CLEANSE AND CHARGE — BASIC CRYSTAL HEALING TECHNIQUES

Before we look at performing specific crystal body layouts, we first must know the basic methods of how to use crystals to cleanse and charge the chakras. While I encourage you to experiment and find a style that works best for you, there are some guidelines that I highly recommend you work to, especially in the early stages of your crystal healing journey.

The following techniques can form the basis of most of your crystal work, regardless of which chakra you are working on, or what healing outcome you want to achieve.

OPEN THE DOOR

The most effective way of removing blocked or unbalanced energy from the energetic body is to work with the natural downflow of energy mentioned earlier in this chapter. Remember that heavy energy migrates down the body and is released through the Root Chakra.

So, whenever we are working on cleansing any chakra in the body, it is essential that we cleanse and open the Root Chakra *first*. This opens the gates of your energy highway in a similar way to opening the front door before you sweep the dirt out.

Let's imagine you are working on releasing a blockage in the Sacral Chakra. If you don't cleanse and open the Root Chakra first, then all the blocked energy you dislodge from the Sacral Chakra will most probably just flow down the energy highway and jam up the Root Chakra, potentially causing a whole other range of problems.

Similarly, the most effective way of energising and charging the chakras is to work with the natural upflow of energy, because light energy rises upwards. Therefore, the Higher Crown Chakra gateway should always be opened and charged *first* when the healing session is focused on charging the chakras.

CLEANSING THE CHAKRAS

To thoroughly cleanse a chakra, begin by holding a wand a couple of inches above the chakra point with the point of the wand directed towards the body. If you are working on a partner, then it will be most comfortable for both of you if they are lying face up on a massage table or bed.

Use smooth circular movements with your wrist and circle the wand in an anti-clockwise direction over the chakra. The circles you create in the air should be similar in size to a large apple. This spiralling motion above the chakra collects energetic debris in the same way that a whirlpool collects leaves in a pond.

Next, sweep the wand in a straight line downwards, through the Root Chakra (towards the Earth Chakra) in one flowing motion. This spiralling and sweeping motion can be repeated several times.

As mentioned, always cleanse and open the Root Chakra *first* when removing blockage from *any* chakra in the body. Also, consider which other chakras the energy blockage may need to pass through before it can be eliminated. For example, if you are clearing a trauma from the Heart Chakra, then you first need to cleanse and open the Root Chakra, followed by the Sacral Chakra and then the Solar Plexus Chakra. This allows any blockage released from the Heart Chakra to flow downwards and be released without obstruction along the way.

Be sure that when you are sweeping your wand downwards, you are pulling the energy down the centre of the abdomen to find release through the Root Chakra. Try not to simply flick it away mindlessly. Remember, we need to give unwanted energy somewhere to flow, rather than just moving it from one part of the body to another.

CHARGING THE CHAKRAS

When working on charging or energising a chakra, do the same as cleansing a chakra, but *in reverse*. First charge the chakra by spiralling

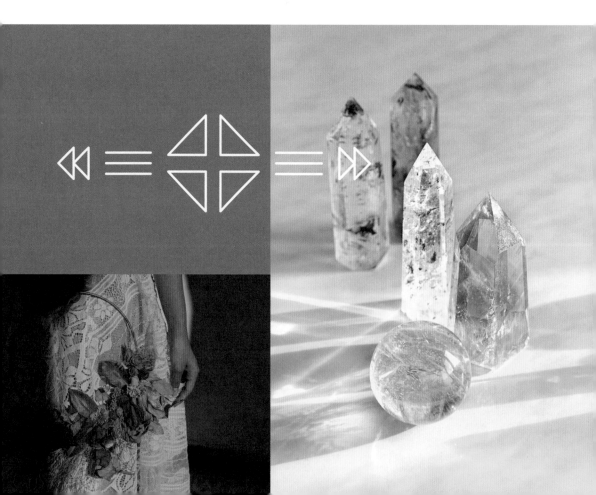

a wand in a clockwise direction over it. Once the chakra feels more energised, sweep the wand upwards along the energy highway to connect with the Higher Crown Chakra. Repeat this as many times as needed.

Always cleanse and open the Higher Crown Chakra *first* when charging and energising *any* chakra in the body. Also, consider which other chakras the energy may need to pass through before it can connect with spirit-energy through the Higher Crown Chakra. For example, if you are working on charging and connecting the Throat Chakra to the Higher Crown Chakra, you first need to open and connect the Crown and Third Eye chakras to the Higher Crown Chakra. This ensures that the energy highway between the Throat and Higher Crown chakras is clear, and the energy can flow freely upwards without getting stuck along the way.

HIGH VIBE OR LOW VIBE

I am often asked whether one should begin a crystal healing at the Earth Chakra or Higher Crown Chakra and whether to work up or down the line of chakras on the body. There seems to be a lot of conflicting information about this (depending on where you get your information from), which can be quite confusing.

As a Spiritual Rebel I don't like limiting myself to a set of rules. Rules take you out of heart and spirit and into the mind, which is not the most intuitive place to be working from in crystal healing!

For this reason, I encourage you to remain flexible and, instead of asking yourself 'How should I be doing this healing?', ask 'What does my partner need to receive from this healing?' or, when practising on yourself, 'What do I need from this healing?'

If a person's energy is heavy and flat from a stressful day at work, then focusing the crystal work on the higher chakras first will lift their vibration and mood instantly. You might also like to leave the crystals longer on the higher chakras.

Alternatively, if a person is in a heightened state of excitement or is feeling edgy and anxious, then beginning the crystal work at the lower chakras will help to bring some much-needed grounding and calmness to their energy.

When in doubt, ensure your focus and intention are on the person receiving the crystal healing (even if that is yourself!) and, from your highest level of consciousness, ask what *they* need from the healing and how you can best serve *their* needs.

EARTH COMES FIRST — CORRECT CRYSTAL PLACEMENT

When I began practising as a newly trained crystal therapist, I soon found that there had been significant gaps in my training: a number of skills that I later learned were important to crystal healing hadn't been taught in the first instance. In many ways, I was left to stumble through as best I could, while I gained experience. Thankfully, I had forgiving clients. They silently encouraged me, while I clumsily dug through their heart-space and crystals rolled off them and fell around us.

One area of knowledge that was completely overlooked was the subtle art of correctly placing crystals on a living, breathing human body. It sounds quite straightforward, doesn't it? Just choose the crystal and place it on the corresponding chakra, right?

Not quite! While it may be fine to place a crystal inside your own underwear to treat the Root Chakra, this would be out of the question with a client in the healing room.

A person with washboard abs might be the perfect canvas for an elaborate Sacral Chakra crystal layout, but how would this same layout work on a larger person or a pregnant woman with a rounded belly? I assure you at least half of those crystals will end up on the floor.

So, before we can master the complexities of full-body crystal layouts, let's take a moment to get the basics right.

When placing crystals on the chakras (or other areas of the body), there are some key things to consider. We need to ensure the crystals have the desired impact, while also staying in place.

We also need to be mindful of personal boundaries when performing crystal healing on another person or in a professional setting. Aim to work respectfully yet effectively, so as not to compromise on the effect of the crystal healing.

People come in all different shapes and sizes. Whether a person is short, tall, round, thin, bony, wide, narrow or somewhere in the middle, we want to make sure that the crystals are placed correctly on the body, and that a back-up strategy is in place when things don't go exactly to plan.

Here are some useful tips for correctly and skilfully placing crystals on the body.

DON'T BE A HELIUM BALLOON

Spiritual seekers and inexperienced crystal therapists commonly make the mistake of focusing *only* on the higher chakras when performing crystal work. And while, yes, crystal healing is a high-vibrational healing modality, Earth always comes first. It is essential to integrate these raised energetic frequencies into the physical, low-vibrational body for true healing results.

No matter how spiritually advanced a person may be, they are still a *person* made of physical matter. They are therefore deeply connected to the physical dimension and earthly energies. Any higher consciousness work we perform on ourselves or others *must* be integrated into the physical body to maintain balance, harmony and equilibrium.

This aligns with the universal principle of correspondence, which states that everything without is echoed within. Similarly, everything within is echoed without. In other words, high-vibrational healing energy must be received and reflected by our low-vibrational physical body to be fully integrated.

In the same way that a helium balloon will float away when its string has been cut from its anchor, a person who is experiencing a fast, spiritual ascension without adequate grounding can become unstable and disconnected from their earthly roots. This may lead them to feel light-headed, foggy, lost, disconnected from work, or out-of-sync with loved ones or their physical life. In extreme cases, they may even experience mental distress or a spiritual crisis. For this reason, it is essential that inexperienced and new crystal healers always include a grounding crystal in their crystal body layouts.

Place a suitable crystal down at Earth Chakra *first*, before placing any other crystals on the body. If you are working with a massage table, then you may also like to place a grounding stone under the table. This will strengthen the energetic connection to Earth and anchor the Earth Chakra.

Appropriate Earth Chakra crystals include Hematite, Obsidian, Brown Agate and Black Tourmaline. If you are working on a tall person whose feet hang off the healing table, then the crystal can be placed between their ankles, instead of below the feet.

Once the Earth Chakra crystal is in place, the next crystal we should place is the Higher Crown Chakra crystal.

Appropriate Higher Crown Chakra crystals include Selenite, Clear Quartz and Clear Calcite. The crystal should be placed above the top of the head, but if your partner's head is at the top of a massage table, then you can tuck it just under the top of their head. If this isn't possible, then you can simply place a large violet or clear crystal on the top of the forehead, which is for the Crown and Higher Crown chakras.

By following these steps, we have essentially opened up the two gateways that feed our energy system: Earth and Spirit. With both gateways open, an even and balanced stream of energy can flow through the body. We are then ready to place the remaining crystals and begin the healing work!

COVER UP

Always lay a sheet or blanket over your partner (or yourself), before placing the crystals. This serves two purposes: the folds of the fabric help to hold the crystals in place and your partner (or you) will feel warm and secure by being covered.

Gently wrinkle and bunch the sheet or blanket around any crystals that seem determined to roll around.

Choose a plain, light-coloured fabric such as white or pale blue, so you can easily see the crystals on top. Try to avoid strong colours such as orange or red, as these can be too stimulating. An exception to this would be if you are working with a person who has described themselves as feeling lethargic and wants to awaken their energy reserves.

RESPECT THE ROOT

If you are performing a crystal healing on yourself, then you can place the Root Chakra crystal directly over the chakra or inside your underwear to sit against your perineum.

However, if you are working with a partner, it is best to place this crystal between the upper thighs, below the groin and above the knees.

The Root Chakra funnel comes out like an upside-down cone from the perineum, reaching down towards the knee region. By placing the crystal between the upper thighs (inside the energy funnel), you are still able to work directly with this chakra, while respecting personal boundaries.

WHERE'S THE BATHROOM — COMMON RESPONSES TO A CRYSTAL HEALING

Crystal healing is an extremely safe and relaxing form of therapy, but that is not to say that a crystal healing session is completely without risk or response.

Because crystals work to penetrate the energetic level of the body, reactions to a crystal healing session can occur at any level: physical, emotional, spiritual or psychological. That said, they are usually minimal and pass within a few hours.

One of the very first crystal healings I performed in a professional setting resulted in a complete emotional breakdown by my client. Midway through the session and during her deepened state, a repressed childhood memory unexpectedly surfaced. She had not dealt with this traumatic experience and had pushed it deeper and deeper down into her subconscious, where it lay forgotten and dormant for over 15 years.

Not anymore.

As a newly qualified crystal therapist, I felt under-prepared for such an emotional breakdown (which was also a breakthrough, though it didn't feel like it at the time). I supported her as best I could with my limited skillset and projected a facade of what was hopefully reassuring confidence.

Inwardly, I was wondering what the fuck I had done.

Fortunately, my skills improved with time and experience, and I learned to educate my clients more thoroughly on what they could expect during and after a crystal healing session. I also became much more competent at guiding my clients through their healing journey.

How a person responds to a crystal healing depends on their sensitivity to crystal energy and how skilled their crystal therapist is. However, although everybody resonates differently with crystals, there are some common responses that most people seem to experience in varying degrees. Before you get started, it is always good practice to explain to your partner or client what they might experience during and after their crystal healing.

Here are some of the most common experiences.

RELAXATION

Most people will sink into a deep state of relaxation during a non-trauma-related crystal healing session (such as a relaxing chakra-balancing session). This is like the energetic and spiritual equivalent of receiving a relaxing body massage and should feel calming and enjoyable.

Afterwards, you might feel as though you have awoken from a deep sleep and you may even feel lightly sedated. This is perfectly normal and usually wears off within the first half-hour. Many people feel a deep sense of calm for the rest of the day.

LIGHT-HEADEDNESS

It is common to feel a little light-headed or a bit 'out of it' immediately after a crystal healing, which is why good grounding is important.

Given that crystals are high-vibrational beings working to lift your frequency into a higher state, sometimes it can take a while for the renewed energetic frequencies to settle into the physical body (which is why you can become light-headed).

If you are feeling a little light-headed after a crystal healing session, drink a glass of water (or herbal tea) and allow yourself a couple of minutes to ground. A pinch of salt to dissolve on the tongue can help speed this up, as will walking around barefoot for a couple of minutes.

HEADACHE

Occasionally, you may experience mild headache or pressure if the crystal healing session has included focused work on the head or higher chakras (such as the Crown or Third Eye chakras). This is normal and is caused by the release of blocked energy.

Just like massaging a knot out of the lower back might result in temporary muscle tenderness, any sudden energetic movement or release can result in temporary discomfort in the treated area. This can take up to 48 hours to pass, but is usually gone after the first couple of hours.

If you or your partner develop a mild headache after receiving a crystal healing, then support it by applying a cool cloth over the forehead, or by gently massaging on some lavender massage oil.

STOMACH/DIGESTIVE DISCOMFORT

When working on the lower energy centres such as the Sacral and Root chakras, you might experience mild digestive discomfort,

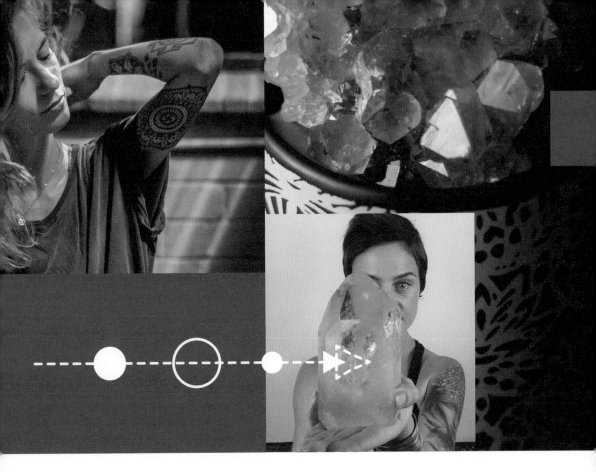

including stomach rumbling, nausea or gas while the crystals are in place. If the session also includes some focused detoxification and cleansing work through the lower chakras, you may find yourself running for the bathroom immediately after the session!

Any concentrated crystal work through the lower chakras can trigger more frequent bowel movements, slightly heavier menstruation and mild nausea for up to 48 hours after the healing. This is all perfectly normal and indicates that the energetic cleanse has been effective in triggering the elimination of toxins from the body.

FEELING EMOTIONAL

Many people find crystal healing to be an intensely emotional experience (especially if the session involves revisiting or releasing energetic trauma).

The energy of the crystals penetrates deep into the subconscious layers to gently find the root of the trauma. This is then drawn out and brought into conscious light for acknowledgement and exploration.

Sometimes, we may even unexpectedly find ourselves face-to-face with repressed memories, which can be quite painful.

If a crystal healing session has left you feeling emotionally raw or vulnerable, make sure you are completely supported and nurtured through this period.

If you are working on a partner who has become emotional, make sure you provide them with a safe and supportive space to explore their feelings. Encourage them to reflect gently on their experience without judgement or opinion.

Please remember that, unless you are a qualified counsellor or psychologist, your role is not to 'counsel' your partner or client. You are there to listen, support and provide them with a nurturing space to explore their feelings.

Crystal healing is a very subtle and gentle healing modality. Any symptoms that you or your partner experience as a direct result of the crystal healing session will only be mild in nature. If you or your partner experience a severe physical reaction after a crystal healing session such as intense pain, diarrhoea, dizziness or vomiting, then you should seek immediate medical assistance. These symptoms are *not* related to the healing and could indicate a more serious underlying medical condition.

Crystal healing is sometimes dismissed as a 'fluffy' New Age healing modality, but, when applied purposefully and intentionally (with more than just a whimsical fancy for pretty, sparkly things), it is a powerful tool to be used for profound personal growth and deep healing.

In the next chapter, I will share with you some of the most powerful crystal healing body layouts I have worked with in my professional practice.

PART

A REBEL'S GUIDE TO CRYSTAL BODY LAYOUTS

AN INTRODUCTION TO CRYSTAL BODY LAYOUTS

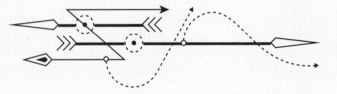

A Spiritual Rebel understands that deep healing is not achieved by being predictable and 'safe'. Healing requires a new perspective, stepping out of one's comfort zone and doing things a different way. I do crystal healing a different way.

Working with my unique skillset and understanding of crystal healing, I have created the following crystal body layouts (sometimes called crystal body grids) to provide healing support for life's most common health issues. The key word here is *support*. I am not touting miracle cures or stand-alone treatments. Crystal healing is a vibrational healing modality, meaning it works alongside the energy of the person being treated. If a person is open and empowered, then the result will most likely be more positive than if a person is sceptical and disempowered.

You do not need to be a professional crystal therapist to use the following body layouts. They have been created as an open resource for you to use as effectively at home on yourself and the family as in a professional healing room. However, please keep in mind that many of the layouts are designed to help support healing through

traumatic situations (such as sexual trauma and depression) and should *not* be used in a professional context unless you are fully qualified to do so.

Finally, remember that you are a Spiritual Rebel with your own knowledge and healing path. While my layouts are provided for your reference, I encourage you to breathe your own energy and style into them, to find what works uniquely for you. Listen to your intuition, trust yourself and let the healing work begin!

GETTING THE MOST FROM EACH LAYOUT

As you now know, there is so much more to performing a crystal healing than simply placing crystals on the chakras and waiting for the magic to happen.

Before starting any crystal work, I like to spend 5–10 minutes guiding my client into a state of relaxation with a meditation. I also adjust their body with a gentle spinal alignment. Once the client is fully surrendered and ready, I place the crystals on their body. With crystals in place, I spend a further 10 minutes setting the intention for the stones by softly placing my hands over each crystal or chakra and sending healing energy into my client.

During the session, I use wands to cleanse, remove and direct energy through the body. I might also incorporate guided visualisation, Reiki, pranic energy healing, essential oils, smudging, aura reading, chakra massage, creative-expressive therapy, ritual or anything else I feel intuitively called to do, while the crystals are in place. This is where my 'no rules' policy really comes into play!

If you are content to stick with the basics for now, here is a great 'starter' formula that can be applied to all the following layouts if you are working on a partner:

1. Get your partner comfortable, lying on their back, with a sheet covering them.

2. Take your partner on a 5-minute guided meditation. This can be as simple as playing a recorded meditation or speaking in a soft voice.

3. Place the crystals on your partner's body. Remember to start with the Earth Chakra crystal, followed by the Higher Crown.

4. Refer back to 'Cleanse and charge' (see page 83). Follow the steps for cleansing the chakras, beginning with the Root Chakra and work up the body. Once all the chakras are cleansed, you can charge them following the steps for charging the chakras.

5. Make sure the crystals remain on your partner for at least 20 minutes.

6. Gently remove the crystals and invite your partner to sit up when they are ready. Offer them a glass of water and encourage them to share their experience with you.

If you are working on yourself, then here are some helpful step-by-step tips:

1. Begin sitting up.

2. Place the Earth Chakra crystal in position between your feet, then lie down. (If you have short arms, then I suggest also placing the Root Chakra crystal at your groin before lying down.)

3. Place the Higher Crown crystal above the top of your head. Once this is in place, you can place the other main crystals on the appropriate points of your body, by feeling your way and tilting your head to look down the length of your body. Place any face crystals (such as for the Third Eye Chakra) last.

4. Once all crystals are in place, then you might like to listen to a guided meditation to help you relax. (Have your phone or music control nearby.)

5. Follow the instructions for cleansing and charging your chakras (see page 83). Once all the chakras are cleansed, you can charge them following the steps for charging the chakras.

6. Make sure the crystals remain on your body for at least 20 minutes.

7. Gently remove the crystals from your face and body first, then you can remove the Higher Crown crystal and finally sit up when you are ready and remove the Earth Chakra crystal. Don't forget to have a glass of water and be as gentle with yourself as you would if you were working on someone else.

SUBSTITUTING CRYSTALS

You will need a range of crystals to replicate the crystal body layouts in this guide. Each stone has been chosen for that exact placement and layout because of its unique healing properties and ability to interact with the other stones in the layout. For this reason, if you are a beginner, I do recommend that you stay true to the exact crystals used in each layout for the best result.

If you do not have access to all the crystals described and need to substitute one or more of the stones, this table lists your alternative crystal options for working at specific chakras.

CHAKRA	COLOUR	SUITABLE CRYSTALS
Higher Crown	White/ Clear	Clear Quartz, Clear Calcite, Selenite, Danburite, Celestite, Azeztulite, Scolecite, Apophyllite, Moonstone
Crown	Violet	Light Amethyst, Purple Fluorite, Purple Calcite, Sugilite, Charoite, Lepidolite, Violet Tanzanite
Third Eye	Indigo	Iolite, Blue Sapphire, Lapis Lazuli, Dark Amethyst, Blue Kyanite, Labradorite, Blue Tanzanite
Throat	Blue	Sodalite, Turquoise, Angelite, Blue Lace Agate, Lapis Lazuli, Blue Topaz, Aquamarine
Heart	Green/ Pink	Green Aventurine, Moss Agate, Malachite, Chrysocolla, Emerald, Rhyolite, Unakite, Green Calcite, Green Fluorite, Jade, Dioptase, Rose Quartz, Rhodonite, Rhodochrosite, Pink Kunzite, Pink Tourmaline, Watermelon Tourmaline, Ruby/Ruby in Zoisite
Solar Plexus	Yellow	Citrine, Amber, Heliodore (Golden Beryl), Yellow Jasper, Yellow Agate, Tiger's Eye, Pyrite
Sacral	Orange	Dark Amber, Carnelian, Fire Agate, Aragonite, Orange Calcite, Orange Jasper, Sunstone
Root	Red	Bloodstone, Red Jasper, Red Agate, Carnelian, Garnet, Muscovite, Red Tiger's Eye
Earth	Black/ Brown	Hematite, Black Tourmaline, Obsidian, Black/Brown Agate, Orthoceras, Smoky Quartz, Shungite, Apache Tears, Jet, Black Onyx

CRYSTAL POINTS

You will find that many of the crystal layouts include the use of Clear Quartz, Amethyst and Citrine points, and occasionally Kyanite blades (which can be used like points). The points are used to direct the flow of energy in the layouts and to amplify the effect of the main healing stones. I have chosen specific types of points for each layout because of their suitability for that particular layout.

If you do not have access to crystal points, then it is possible to leave them out of the layout. It is also possible to substitute Amethyst and Citrine points with Clear Quartz points if necessary.

CRYSTALS NOT TO BE SUBSTITUTED

While it is okay to substitute some crystals in a layout, it is recommended that you do not substitute any stones that are on the focal chakra for the layout (especially if you are a beginner and are unfamiliar with the healing properties of individual stones). For example, if Rose Quartz is on the Heart Chakra in a layout that focuses on emotional trauma, then it should not be substituted. It has been specifically chosen because of its unique properties for working on that chakra. If the Rose Quartz is placed on the Heart Chakra in a layout that does *not* focus on the heart (in a general chakra layout, for example) then it may be substituted with one of the other suggested stones.

Some crystals that should not be substituted if possible include Rainbow Quartz, Malachite, Orthoceras, Selenite, Shiva Lingam, Moldavite, Moonstone, Kyanite and Smoky Quartz. This is because they hold unique healing properties not found in other stones or they have unique origins.

CRYSTAL BODY LAYOUTS

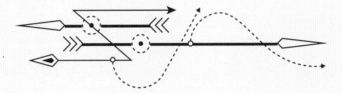

The following layouts have been organised in order of most simple to most complex depending on how many crystals are used and the nature of the healing to be done. For example, performing a layout to support lower back pain requires less skill and knowledge than performing a layout for someone who has depression. I recommend sticking to the basics until you feel confident progressing to the more challenging layouts. Part of being a Spiritual Rebel is knowing yourself, which means knowing and respecting where you are at with your personal and professional development (see next page).

As you work through the following crystal body layouts, you will find expert tips to help take your healing skills to the next level. The tips are layout-specific, meaning they have been recommended for that particular layout and have been practised in my own healing room. However, you will find that sometimes the same tips work for multiple body layouts.

PROFESSIONAL TRAINING

Please work only within your qualifications and experience if you are performing these layouts on another person or in a professional setting. It is important to keep in mind that this book does *not* constitute professional crystal healing training. If you *are* considering becoming a professional crystal healing practitioner, then please visit my online crystal healing training academy, Evolve Healing Institute, evolvehealing.net/crystal-healing-courses. Here you will find several internationally accredited and professional crystal healing practitioner training courses to suit all ability levels.

You will also find that each layout includes a difficulty level, an outline of the healing outcomes, an illustrated diagram and helpful details about the layout, the crystals chosen and the healing goal. While the descriptions are written from the perspective of working on a partner, all of these layouts can be performed on yourself, using the modification suggestions on page 103.

CHAKRA BALANCE

HEALING OUTCOMES

Balance | Cleansing | Refreshment | Alignment | Relaxation | Peace

DIFFICULTY LEVEL

Easy

CRYSTAL PLACEMENT

EARTH:	Hematite
CROWN:	Selenite (natural stick preferred)
THIRD EYE:	Sugilite
THROAT:	Sodalite
HEART:	Rose Quartz
SOLAR PLEXUS:	Citrine
SACRAL:	Carnelian
ROOT:	Bloodstone

CRYSTAL POINTS

» **None**

THE HEALING

The goal for this layout is to provide an energetic healing that is very well balanced and also to bring the qualities of alignment, cleansing and relaxation to all levels of being.

This is not a crystal healing aimed at triggering an intense emotional response, nor is it meant to target buried energetic trauma. It is instead a beautifully calming layout – the equivalent of a spa treatment for the energetic body. Ideally, your partner will 'float' off the bed afterwards, with a deep and blissful feeling of relaxation!

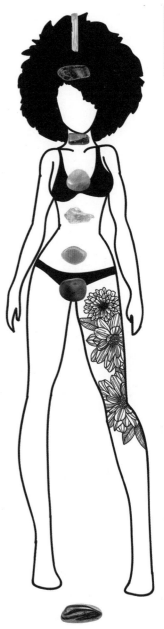

Selenite at the Crown Chakra works to balance the astral energies and bring alignment in a downwards flowing direction through all the chakras. It clears away any negative programming and thoughts, replacing these with calmness and openness. This helps re-establish a connection to the Divine, so messages and inspiration can flow freely through the Crown Chakra.

Sugilite at the Third Eye Chakra instils an even deeper sense of calm and tranquillity, slowing down busy thoughts. It works with the Selenite to enhance intuition and wisdom.

We use Sodalite at the Throat Chakra to help open and support self-expression, communication and clarity. It also works to cleanse this area and open the pathway of connection between the Heart and Third Eye chakras. This helps us to understand and transform our emotional truth into a higher, intuitive vibration.

At the Heart Chakra, Rose Quartz brings gentle, emotionally balancing healing energy. The key word here is gentle; Rose Quartz supports and nurtures as it does its emotional healing work. It softly penetrates the deepest emotional layers to reveal our highest potential for forgiveness, love, compassion and empathy.

Citrine at the Solar Plexus Chakra brings positivity, light, confidence and joy. This amazing feel-good energy flows throughout the entire energy highway and washes away energetic heaviness or negativity.

At the lower chakras, we use a cleansing combination of Bloodstone and Carnelian to help release any blocked or toxic energy and bring balance and healing to the lower spine and digestive system.

The magnetic force of Hematite at the Earth Chakra pulls this blockage downwards and out of the body for release.

EXPERT TIPS

◊   A great way to make sure that all crystals are in alignment is to stand at the head of your partner once you have placed all the stones and look down the length of their body. The crystals should be in a straight line down the chakras. Feel free to make any adjustments to create perfect crystal alignment.

◊   Ask your partner to visualise a beam of warm, white light flowing in through their Higher Crown Chakra. Encourage them to feel it flowing down, through the centre of their body, flushing away anything that doesn't serve them.

◊   Place your hands gently over each chakra point and send your healing intentions into your partner's body.

CONFIDENCE AND SELF-ESTEEM

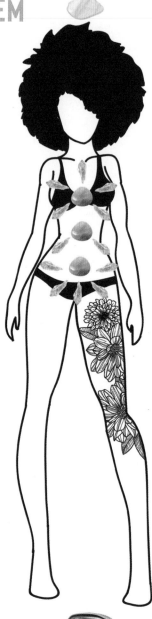

HEALING OUTCOMES

Confidence | Self-acceptance | Self-love | Self-forgiveness |
Self-esteem | Positivity

DIFFICULTY LEVEL

Easy

CRYSTAL PLACEMENT

EARTH:	Grounding stone of choice (Obsidian, Hematite, Shungite, for example)
HIGHER CROWN:	Higher stone of choice (Clear Quartz, Selenite, Clear Calcite, for example)
HEART:	Rose Quartz
SOLAR PLEXUS:	Rose Quartz
SACRAL:	Rose Quartz

CRYSTAL POINTS

» 8–14 Citrine points placed around the Heart, Solar Plexus and Sacral chakras, pointing inwards.

THE HEALING

This is one of the simplest yet most profound of all the layouts in this book. Some crystals simply love working together, and Citrine and Rose Quartz make a powerful pair!

Rose Quartz is a gentle yet effective healer. At the Heart Chakra, it works to support the emotions and open the heart, so we can give and receive love in giant proportions. It also encourages forgiveness and acceptance of ourselves and others.

At the Solar Plexus Chakra, Rose Quartz reminds us of our inner strength and ability to love. This helps to foster self-confidence and trust in our abilities and acceptance of perceived imperfections (such as our flaws).

At the Sacral Chakra, it reminds us to love all that we are, especially our physical body. It helps us to release judgement of our appearance and things we cannot change, such as events in our past that may have had a lasting influence on our life.

Citrine is the ultimate stone for light, positivity, joy, inspiration and abundance. It resonates most strongly with the Solar Plexus Chakra, but in this layout brings those qualities to each chakra, amplifying and strengthening the properties of the Rose Quartz.

Citrine's golden light helps to chase away all shadows, removing negative programming, non-serving emotions, judgemental feelings, self-hatred, addiction, depression and darkness.

EXPERT TIPS

◊ Any focused Heart Chakra and Solar Plexus Chakra work can be very emotional. Always have tissues on hand and provide as much support as possible to your partner during and after the session. You can do this by encouraging them to talk about their experience of the session and offering them a cup of tea. Remember, your role is not to counsel or offer opinions, but to provide a safe space and to listen and support.

◊ Strengthen the energies of the Rose Quartz by pointing your wand tip at the Citrine points and trace along their length, towards the Heart, Solar Plexus and Sacral chakras.

◊ Ask your partner to visualise a gold-coloured energy ball warming their heart-space from within. Ask them to visualise it growing bigger, stronger and warmer, shining light throughout their whole body, filling them with a deep sense of love, joy and acceptance.

◊   In my experience, those who have low self-esteem may not experience much touch from others. Not only will adding touch to this session help to anchor and infuse the heart-healing into the body, but it will also offer your partner a powerful restorative experience. Try gently placing your hands over your partner's Heart, Solar Plexus and Sacral chakras in turn. Close your eyes and focus on sending all your love and healing energy into these energy centres. Flat chakra stones are ideal in this layout, because you can easily place your hands over them.

◊   It can be a beautiful experience for your partner to recite a positive mantra, such as 'I am worthy of giving and receiving love' during this layout.

CLEANSING AND DETOXIFICATION

HEALING OUTCOMES

Energetic and physical detoxification | Processing energetic trauma | Overcoming energetic blocks | Emotional release | Improved digestion | Relief from constipation, low libido and bloating | Cleansing and healing of the lower chakras | Release of non-serving patterns

DIFFICULTY LEVEL

Easy

CRYSTAL PLACEMENT

EARTH:	Grounding stone of choice (Hematite works well in this layout)
HIGHER CROWN:	Higher stone of choice (Clear Quartz, Selenite, Clear Calcite, for example)
SOLAR PLEXUS:	Carnelian
SACRAL:	Bloodstone
ROOT:	Hematite

CRYSTAL POINTS

» 10–15 Clear Quartz points placed around the lower chakras. They should all point inwards and be angled down towards the Root Chakra.

THE HEALING

This is another simple but powerful healing grid. It is my favourite when working on energy blocks that have been lodged in the lower chakras for a long time.

Carnelian, Bloodstone and Hematite are all intensely cleansing crystals. They work perfectly together to draw out energetic blockage and toxicity in the lower chakras and replace these with a feeling of more energy and 'charge'. Energy blocks include emotional trauma (which we experience energetically through the Heart Chakra but often hold in the Sacral Chakra), feelings of self-loathing (usually felt in the Solar Plexus Chakra) and any issues surrounding sexuality, body image, physical injury and the digestive organs (felt through the Sacral and Root chakras).

We place Hematite at the Root Chakra in this layout, because its natural magnetic forces pull all the energy downwards for release.

Just like when we detoxify physically (such as with a juice cleanse), energetic waste is eliminated through the Root Chakra by way of the organs of elimination. Because of this, your partner may experience stomach gurgling, gas or the urge to use the bathroom during or immediately after this crystal layout.

Clear Quartz points help to cleanse, enhance and direct the flow of energy downwards through the Root Chakra.

EXPERT TIPS

◊ Be sure to let your partner know that they may experience mild stomach discomfort or digestive disturbance for up to 48 hours after this layout. This is perfectly normal and indicates the session has been effective.

◊ Amplify the effect of the detoxification stones by pointing your wand tip at the Quartz points and trace lines along their length, towards the Solar Plexus, Sacral and Root chakras.

◊ Use your wand (or pendulum) to draw the energy downwards and out through the Root Chakra.

◊ It is important that your partner drinks lots of water and does not consume any processed food or alcohol for 48 hours after the session. This will help to maximise the energetic cleanse process.

SLEEP

HEALING OUTCOMES

Deeper, better quality sleep | Calming an overactive mind | Encourages vivid dreams | Faster transition through jetlag | Stabilising disrupted sleep patterns (in shift workers, for example)

DIFFICULTY LEVEL

Easy

CRYSTAL PLACEMENT

EARTH:	Smoky Quartz
HIGHER CROWN:	Selenite
CROWN:	Moonstone
THIRD EYE:	Sodalite

CRYSTAL POINTS

» 2–4 Amethyst points placed around the top of the head. They should all point in towards the head.

» 2–4 Clear Quartz points placed around the top of the head, pointing away from the head.

THE HEALING

Often, insomnia is caused by a psychological issue such as stress, fear, anxiety or an inability to switch off. However, it is important to make sure that sleeplessness is not due to a physiological issue, such as sleep apnoea, as this would require a different type of crystal layout (and possibly medical treatment).

For this layout, I prefer to use Selenite at the Higher Crown Chakra. Not only is Selenite extremely gentle and calming, but it is also wonderful for protecting against unwanted entities and releasing negative energetic 'debris' stuck in the aura. It will help to ward off bad dreams and will assist empaths in letting go of unwanted energy that they may have picked up through the day.

At the Crown Chakra, Moonstone connects us to the lunar energies. It helps to align our consciousness with the ebb and flow of the natural circadian night-time rhythms.

Moonstone is also excellent for calming and quietening a busy mind, as well as alleviating any night-time fears. It holds the gentle, nurturing energy of the Divine Feminine, which creates a feeling of comfort and safety, supporting us like a mother supports a baby who is ready to drift into a deep sleep.

Sodalite at the Third Eye offers calm, clarity and stillness. It is a little more forceful than Moonstone in this regard, as it contains more masculine energy. The two stones work beautifully together to bring an overall feeling of deep tranquillity and mental relief.

Amethyst points are in place around the top of the head to channel pure peace energy into the psyche in preparation for the surrender to sleep. Amethyst is an extremely tranquil and mystical stone, working to alleviate fears, stress, anxiety, restlessness and insecurities that may be affecting our ability to switch off at night. It facilitates the 'sinking' into a profound level of consciousness, ensuring that we not only sleep, but sleep deeply.

While Amethyst channels energy inwards, Clear Quartz carries energy outwards, acting as a conduit for us to release any stress or energetic blockage that

USING OILS AND FRAGRANCES

An important note when working with oils, incense and fragrances (to be kept in mind for all layouts that suggest the application of these products): always ask your partner if they have any sensitivities to oils or incense *before* using these products in the healing room or applying them to their skin (or on fabric that is in contact with their skin). Some people dislike the smell and may even have an allergic physical reaction to these products.

may be affecting our sleep health. Clear Quartz penetrates deep into all levels of our energetic body to cleanse, heal and carry away all that no longer serves.

At the Earth Chakra, we use Smoky Quartz, because of its grounding, cleansing and stabilising qualities. It holds the energy of clarity and not only helps to calm a restless body, but also to clear a busy and cluttered mind.

EXPERT TIPS

◊ This layout is best performed immediately before bedtime in a quiet, dimly lit space. This will ensure you or your partner are able to fully relax and can effortlessly transition from a deep, meditative healing state to a restful sleep state.

◊ Amplify the effect of the crystal points by pointing a wand tip at each of the Amethyst and Quartz points and trace lines along their length in the direction they are pointing.

◊ Massage a couple of drops of lavender or frankincense massage oil into your partner's temples and Third Eye before placing the stones down. Alternatively, you may like to add a couple of drops to a purple or indigo cloth, then cover your partner's eyes with the cloth. You can place the crystals over the top of the cloth. (See note on facing page.)

◊ Take your partner through a deeply relaxing guided meditation to help them fully immerse in this experience. Invite them to relax their muscles and disengage from any distraction and clutter in the mind. This will encourage the whole body to release and surrender.

◊ Invite your partner to place Selenite, Moonstone and Amethyst crystals under their pillow at night to have the continued benefit of these stones as they sleep.

PERIOD PAIN AND PREMENSTRUAL SYNDROME (PMS)

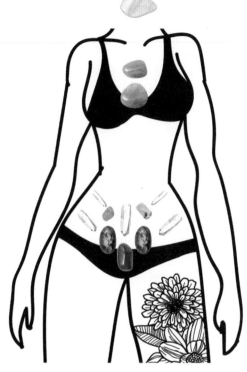

HEALING OUTCOMES

Relief from period pain and discomfort | Relief from PMS symptoms | Relief from ovulation discomfort | Support through hormonal mood swings

DIFFICULTY LEVEL

Easy

CRYSTAL PLACEMENT

EARTH:	Grounding stone of choice (Obsidian, Shungite, Hematite, for example)
HIGHER CROWN:	Higher stone of choice (Clear Quartz, Selenite, Clear Calcite, for example)
HIGHER HEART:	Green Aventurine placed just above the Heart Chakra
HEART:	Rose Quartz
UTERUS:	Red Jasper placed directly over the uterus
OVARIES:	Labradorite placed directly over each ovary
	Green Fluorite placed just above one ovary
	Chrysoprase placed just above the other ovary

CRYSTAL POINTS

» 4–8 Clear Quartz points placed around the uterus and ovaries. Make sure these point towards the organs and are angled downwards.

THE HEALING

This layout is multi-dimensional in that it is designed to target several specific issues related to period discomfort all at once.

At the Higher Heart and Heart chakras, Green Aventurine and Rose Quartz work to soothe and stabilise the emotions.

Rose Quartz is soft, supportive and nurturing, which will help to relieve feelings of sadness and tearfulness. It also helps to take the edge off emotions such as irritability and anger, which can be associated with PMS.

Green Aventurine brings cooling energy to fiery emotions, calming and balancing hormone-related emotional outbursts.

Chrysoprase and Green Fluorite are both cooling and soothing stones, which help in calming heat and inflammation in the body. When placed directly over the affected reproductive areas, they can assist in reducing swelling in the lower belly and lessen period pain.

Labradorite is usually reserved for use at the higher chakras; however, it is a true superstar when treating pain and inflammation specifically related to menstruation. Labradorite over each ovary infuses this area with the energy of the Divine Feminine, supporting these organs through the cleansing process and bringing fast pain relief.

We use Red Jasper over the uterus and near the Root Chakra to support the cleansing process by way of the menstrual blood. Red Jasper subtly but effectively draws the energies downwards, helping the body to purge and release any blocked energy. We don't want to use a 'stronger' cleansing stone here, because we don't want to be overly aggressive in treating what is already an inflamed and uncomfortable area. Red Jasper is a much better choice than Bloodstone or Hematite for this layout specifically because it is more nurturing. It is also excellent for supporting sexual and reproductive health.

Clear Quartz points are angled around the layout, pointing downwards, to really carry this energetic and physical release out through the Root Chakra. Clear Quartz also has the added benefit of being healing and cleansing and can also be effective in drawing pain out of the body.

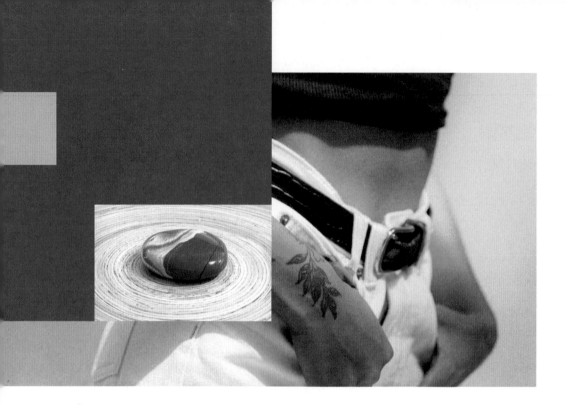

EXPERT TIPS

◊   Heat can help to relieve period pain, so place a heat pack or hot-water bottle over the tender areas while the crystals are in place. This will also help the tense muscles to relax, allowing a better flow of energy to penetrate and be absorbed from the crystals.

◊   Place your flat hands (palms facing down) over your partner's ovaries, sending warmth and healing energy into this space.

◊   For period pain that wraps around the hips and lower back, you can place crystals on your partner while she is lying face-down.

◊   All these suggestions can easily be performed on yourself too. Follow the modifications on page 103.

ANXIETY AND STRESS

HEALING OUTCOMES

Relief from stress, anxiety and panic attacks | Release of obsessive or overwhelming thoughts | Mental clarity and perspective | Relief from stress-induced headaches | Calming an overactive mind

DIFFICULTY LEVEL

Easy

CRYSTAL PLACEMENT

EARTH:	Grounding stone of choice (Hematite, Obsidian, Shungite, for example)
HIGHER CROWN:	Clear Quartz
CROWN:	Amethyst
THIRD EYE:	Sodalite
HIGHER HEART:	Amazonite
HEART:	Rose Quartz

CRYSTAL POINTS

» 4 small Amethyst points placed around the Crown and Third Eye chakras. These should all point in towards the chakras.
» 4–6 Clear Quartz points placed around the top of the head, pointing away from the head.
» 2–4 Clear Quartz points placed around the Heart Chakra. These should point in towards the heart.

THE HEALING

In this layout, we harness the cleansing and healing properties of Clear Quartz.

By placing the points around the top of the head facing outwards, we are drawing unwanted energy (such as negative and stressful thoughts) out of the head, leaving clarity and spaciousness in its place.

Amethyst at the Crown Chakra infuses a tranquil and almost meditative consciousness into the brain-space. This helps us to connect with our deepest intuition and knowing.

Paired with calming Sodalite at the Third Eye, these two stones work harmoniously together to quieten disturbing thoughts and unsettling, anxious energy. They are also an effective team when it comes to alleviating stress-induced headaches.

By supporting the Crown and Third Eye chakras with Amethyst points, we amplify this calming, spiritual energy and deliver it straight into the head. This offers relief for anxiety and stress-related symptoms.

Amazonite cleanses the Higher Heart, protecting against irrational emotional responses with balanced energy.

At the Heart Chakra, Rose Quartz brings emotional support, healing and love. It also reminds us to be gentle on ourselves during challenging times.

Together, Rose Quartz and Amazonite work in the heart-space to help calm a fluttery or nervous disposition. They can also be beneficial when it comes to working through nervous jitters that are brought on from panic or anxiety.

This effect is amplified and supported by the surrounding Clear Quartz points.

EXPERT TIPS

◊ Draw stressful and anxious thoughts away from the mind by tracing along the length of the Quartz points around your partner's head with your wand. Visualise smoky threads of vapour being drawn out of the mind as you 'pull' the stress out along the Clear Quartz points and release it.

◊ Once the crystals are in place, ask your partner to visualise themselves being surrounded by soft purple or blue light. Take them through a guided meditation aimed at calming the mind and relaxing the body.

◊ Massage a couple of drops of lavender or frankincense massage oil into your partner's temples and Third Eye before placing the stones down. Alternatively, you may like to add a couple of drops to a purple or indigo cloth, then cover your partner's eyes with the cloth. You can place the crystals over the top of the cloth. (See note on p. 118.)

◊ Any focused work on the head area can result in a mild headache, which may last up to 48 hours. Please be mindful of this and be sure to prepare and support your partner if this occurs.

◊ Light purple and blue are the best colours to use when channelling calming energy. You may incorporate more of these colours into the session by placing a light blue or purple sheet over your partner.

MEDITATION

HEALING OUTCOMES

Mentally 'switching off' | Deepened meditation experience | Heightened intuition | Heightened visionary experience | Release of distracting or busy thoughts

DIFFICULTY LEVEL

Easy

CRYSTAL PLACEMENT

EARTH:	Grounding stone of choice (preferably Orthoceras, Hematite or Smoky Quartz)
HIGHER CROWN:	Clear Quartz
CROWN:	Moonstone
THIRD EYE:	Blue Kyanite

CRYSTAL POINTS

» 2–4 small Amethyst points placed around the Crown and Third Eye chakras. These should all point in towards the chakras.

» 4–8 Clear Quartz and Amethyst points placed around the top of the head, pointing inwards towards the head.

THE HEALING

This layout is incredibly high-vibe, so it is important to use an effective grounding stone (such as Orthoceras, Hematite or Smoky Quartz) to keep your partner anchored. This will help to reduce feelings of light-headedness during and after the session.

I prefer to use Smoky Quartz at the Earth Chakra in this layout, because not only is it a powerful grounding stone, but also it acts as an excellent facilitator for deep meditation and mental clarity.

Clear Quartz at the Higher Crown opens the gateway to the higher spiritual realms. Because Clear Quartz can be programmed through visualisation and meditation, it can work with you to help deliver and enhance specific meditation outcomes.

For example, if you are meditating on manifesting a new job opportunity, you can send this intention into the Clear Quartz crystal *before* you begin the meditation. This intention will be carried and amplified by the Quartz throughout the meditation.

Clear Quartz is also used to clear the mind of mental clutter, bringing clarity and a deeper understanding of universal consciousness.

Moonstone at the Crown Chakra is calming and mystical. It is a stone for the celestial energies and for night. When used on the higher chakras, it brings a sense of soft sedation and peaceful sleep to the waking consciousness.

Moonstone also softens the energies of Blue Kyanite, which is quite effective (but strong) when opening the Third Eye Chakra.

When placed at the higher chakras, Kyanite facilitates communication with higher beings. It helps to enhance visionary ability and truth-seeking and may be a little overwhelming for some who are unfamiliar with its powerful strength. Moonstone helps to transform the powerful (and sometimes overwhelming) visionary experience of the Kyanite into a softer, dream-like meditation experience.

Amethyst is one of the most beneficial crystals for meditation. It quietens and calms the mind and opens the gateways to the higher chakras, so we can connect with our higher consciousness.

Used around the head and at the forehead, Amethyst not only brings these qualities to the meditation, but also enhances the energetic properties of the other crystals in the layout. It is peaceful and serene and will gently guide your journey into the deepest states of consciousness.

Clear Quartz points around the top of the head provide clear channels for the higher energies to flow into the body without obstruction and with clear intention.

EXPERT TIPS

◊   Work with a wand or pendulum to stimulate the Crown and Higher Crown chakras by spiralling your wand in a clockwise direction over these chakras.

Not only will this amplify the energies of the crystals, but it will work to help energetically guide your partner into a more relaxed state. The spiralling movement is quite hypnotic and, although your partner's eyes will be closed, they will still receive the energetic benefit of this movement.

◊   Take your partner through a guided visualisation or meditation to help them sink as deeply as possible into this experience. Include imagery that contains the colours indigo and violet (such as balls of indigo light or violet lotus flowers).

◊   Massage a couple of drops of lavender or frankincense massage oil into your partner's temples and Third Eye before placing the stones down. Alternatively, you may like to add a couple of drops to a purple or indigo cloth, then cover your partner's eyes with the cloth. You can place the crystals over the top of the cloth. (See note on p. 118.)

◊   Any focused work on the head area can result in a mild headache, which may last up to 48 hours. Please be mindful of this and be sure to prepare and support your partner if this occurs.

◊   Light purple and blue are the best colours to use when channelling calming energy. You may incorporate more of these colours into the session by placing a light blue or purple sheet over your partner.

BACK PAIN

HEALING OUTCOMES

Relief from mild or chronic back pain (unrelated to injury) |
Support for spine health | Relief from symptoms associated with
scoliosis and mild arthritis in the spine | Relief from neck pain |
Soothing mild inflammation in the back muscles

DIFFICULTY LEVEL

Easy

CRYSTAL PLACEMENT

For this layout, ask your partner to lie on their stomach, so that
you can place the crystals down the back of the body. It is best to
use a proper massage table in this layout to maintain the integrity
of the neck and spine in this face-down position. You may also like
to place a supportive pillow under your partner's shins or ankles.

EARTH: Black Tourmaline (natural stick preferred)
HIGHER CROWN: Selenite (natural stick preferred)
SPINE: 4–10 Blue Kyanite blades (the number
                    depends on size; blades should run down
                    the entire length of the spine from the base
                    of the head to the Sacral Chakra area)
ROOT: Orthoceras placed vertically over the
                    tailbone in alignment with the Root Chakra

CRYSTAL POINTS

» None

THE HEALING

This layout is designed for maximum alignment and spinal health. Unlike many of
the other layouts included in this book, the crystals described in this layout should be
exactly the type mentioned and should not be substituted.

Selenite, Tourmaline and Kyanite all have a striated cellular structure. This means that the crystal's structure is naturally linear and will usually have visible structural lines or layers.

The reason why we should use the natural stick variety of these crystals is because we really want to enhance and maximise their alignment properties. The natural stick form of the crystal provides a nice long pathway for this linear energy to flow along. A small, tumbled stone would not be quite as effective in embodying and amplifying this linear alignment energy.

We use Selenite at the Higher Crown Chakra and Black Tourmaline at the Earth Chakra to honour astral and earthly energies respectively. Also, the additional lengthening and aligning properties that each stone brings ensures that we have created balanced anchor points between which the spine sits.

Good spinal health depends greatly on good energetic alignment and balance through the central meridian line of the body. If energy is unbalanced within the body, or our astral and earthly anchor points are not properly aligned, then this can create disease and a symptomatic response in the spine.

Blue Kyanite is a natural spine healer. It draws the energies upwards along the spinal pathway to connect us to the higher realms. It resonates with the bones (especially the vertebrae) and brings cleansing, balance and alignment to the physical body as well as the energetic body and chakras.

Placed along the length of the spine, Kyanite cools and soothes, relieving inflammation, while drawing the spine into energetic alignment.

The odd one out here is Orthoceras. Orthoceras is technically not a crystal, but a 400-million-year-old fossil and prehistoric relative of the squid.

Orthoceras is a powerful grounding stone, which we use to achieve profound results in healing energetic trauma in a person's family history (even from past lives). I am a huge fan of this incredible fossil and highly recommend you invest in a couple of specimens in various sizes for your crystal collection. For now, we will focus only on the alignment properties of Orthoceras in this layout.

Because it is a grounding stone, Orthoceras is usually placed on the Root Chakra or Earth Chakra. The geometric patterns we see in the fossil are the spine bones of the animal. For this reason, it is best that we use a piece that has near-perfect alignment and the entire fossil intact, so that the nature of this alignment can permeate your partner's energy field.

Placed on the lower spine, Orthoceras works to align the vertebrae and draw the energies earthwards.

We now have equal energetic forces acting like magnets, subtly pulling the body's energy in opposing directions (downwards towards Earth and upwards towards Spirit). This magnetic pull works on the energetic spine like traction works on the physical spine. It helps to stretch out compression in the energetic body and create length and alignment along the spine. In this spaciousness, imbalance can correct itself and healing can be found.

EXPERT TIPS

◊   Place the palm of one hand on the top of your partner's head (over the Higher Crown Chakra) and place your other palm at the base of your partner's spine (at the Root Chakra). Spend at least 3 minutes with your hands in this placement, visualising the flow of energy running up and down your partner's spine, connecting with both points. Your hands will begin to heat up with energy, which will strengthen the magnetic effect of these two anchor points.

◊   Heat can help to relieve back pain but should be used with caution because some injuries are better treated with cool compression. If it is safe to do so, place a warm towel or heat pack along your partner's spine, over the top of the crystals. This will help to relax the muscles, so that they can absorb the crystals' energies more effectively.

◊   For a quick fix for mild back pain on yourself, use surgical tape or a large band-aid to tape a piece of Kyanite directly over the spine (ask a partner to do this for you if you can't reach). Make sure it is running up and down (in the same direction as the spine), not sideways. The Kyanite can be left on for days (you can shower with it on) and is most effective for treating more localised back pain, such as minor inflammation or muscle strain. Do not do this with Selenite, however, as Selenite is damaged by water.

HEADACHE

HEALING OUTCOMES

Relief from tension and stress headache | Relief from sinus pain and pressure | Relief from eye strain

DIFFICULTY LEVEL

Easy

CRYSTAL PLACEMENT

EARTH:	Grounding stone of choice (Hematite, Obsidian, Shungite, for example)
HIGHER CROWN:	Clear Quartz
CROWN:	Amethyst
THIRD EYE:	Sodalite
EYES:	Lapis Lazuli placed over each closed eyelid
TEMPLES:	Use two smooth Rose Quartz crystals to gently massage each temple

CRYSTAL POINTS

» 4–6 Amethyst points placed around the top of the head, pointing inwards towards the head.

» 4–6 Clear Quartz points placed around the top of the head, pointing away from the head.

THE HEALING

This layout is very relaxing and designed to provide relaxation and gentle pain relief for headaches and migraines.

It is crucial that you use stones that are smooth and comfortable to press against the skin in this layout, especially over the delicate eye area and for massaging around the temples. Choose tumbled or polished stones with no sharp points or rough edges.

Amethyst is a stone of tranquillity and peace. It resonates most deeply with the Crown and Third Eye chakras, relieving discomfort and pressure in the head and brain

area. It helps to replace stressful thoughts with serenity and soothes sharp pain that may be present during a headache.

Sodalite and Lapis Lazuli are cooling stones, carrying the energies of healing blue. Together, they work to release energetic pressure and heat in the head area, while reducing feelings of anxiety, stress, tension and pain.

Sodalite can be beneficial for filtering electromagnetic pollution. This quality makes it ideal for relieving headaches caused by prolonged mobile phone and computer use.

Lapis Lazuli over each eyelid is like having a cool cloth over the eyes. It helps to relax and release tension in the eye area and replaces the hot, throbbing energy of headache with cool, soothing blue energy.

Rose Quartz, while normally used around the Heart Chakra, is also effective in reducing head pain. Use a smooth and polished Rose Quartz crystal over each temple to gently massage the area in a slow circular motion. You can also gently draw the Rose Quartz up over the face, along the jawline and around the eye sockets to release and relax the face muscles on an energetic and physical level.

Clear Quartz points are angled around the top of the head (pointing outwards) to siphon pain and tension from the brain. Clear Quartz points are effective conduits of heat and can be used to draw out pain from any area of the body. For this reason, try to place the points as closely as possible to the actual site of the pain.

Amethyst points (pointing towards the head) are used to channel calming, peaceful energy down through the Higher Crown Chakra into the head. Once the headache subsides, this Amethyst energy will help to ensure your partner has a deep and restful sleep after the session.

EXPERT TIPS

◊ Place your flat palms over each eye, visualising cool water flowing out of them and into your partner.

◊ Use a suitable wand (preferably Clear Quartz, Rose Quartz or Amethyst) to draw the pain and heat out along the Clear Quartz points around the top of the head.

◊ Spiral your wand anti-clockwise over each crystal on the face, then pull the wand upwards, away from the body. This will help to pull out the pain and blocked energy, relieving inflammation and pressure in these areas.

◊ A touch of a carrier oil such as olive or coconut at each temple, with some lavender essential oil, will really help to amplify this session and allows you to glide the Rose Quartz over the skin with more ease. (See note on p. 118.)

◊ Make sure the room is as dark as possible (but not so dark that you can't see the crystals!) and keep noise to a minimum. You may choose not to play music for this session.

◊ Place a chilled cloth over your partner's eyes and change it every 5 minutes. Most migraine sufferers prefer a dark, quiet room with a cool cloth over their eyes for relief.

BALANCE AND ALIGNMENT

HEALING OUTCOMES

General feeling of wellness | Whole body relaxation |
Feeling more centred, focused, balanced and aligned

DIFFICULTY LEVEL

Intermediate

CRYSTAL PLACEMENT

EARTH:	Hematite
HIGHER CROWN:	Selenite (natural stick preferred)
CROWN:	Clear Quartz
THIRD EYE:	Sugilite
THROAT:	Sodalite
HEART:	Rose Quartz
SOLAR PLEXUS:	Citrine
SACRAL:	Carnelian
ROOT:	Bloodstone

CRYSTAL POINTS

» Rather than using points in this layout, we use 5–8
   small to medium Blue Kyanite blades that have at least
   one end with a finely pointed tip. Place one Kyanite
   blade vertically *between* each chakra (so that the
   blades are running in alignment with the chakras,
   rather than cutting across the body horizontally).
   Point the sharpest tip of the blade downwards for a
   more cleansing experience, and upwards for a more
   energising experience.

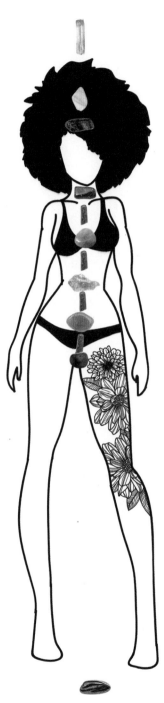

THE HEALING

This layout is a more advanced variation of the Chakra Balance layout covered earlier with the addition of Blue Kyanite blades for enhancing energy flow and alignment between the chakras.

There are many different combinations of crystals you can use when creating this grid. However, I have chosen the following stones because of their wonderful healing properties and easy availability. Together, they work harmoniously to cleanse, balance and align the chakras for fantastic results.

Selenite at the Higher Crown and Clear Quartz at the Crown bring higher consciousness and connection to Spirit.

Selenite is an aligning stone, drawing imbalances into harmony and working on the highest level to cleanse, protect and fill each level of being with white healing light.

The striated crystal form of Selenite resonates with the spine and pulls the energies into a straight arrangement. This creates energetic alignment in the aura.

At the Third Eye Chakra, Sugilite brings soft healing energy and encourages feelings of universal love, acceptance and spiritual awakening. It helps us to identify areas in our life that may be causing imbalance and disharmony, so that we can understand and release them.

Sodalite at the Throat Chakra cleanses, calms and connects us to our inner world of truth and knowing. It helps to settle any imbalance and disturbance in the mind and throat areas, while providing clarity and soothing energy when life becomes a little 'frazzling'.

At the Heart Chakra, Rose Quartz helps to balance and heal the emotional realm, clearing the way for forgiveness and acceptance to occur. Its gentle support allows us to release any emotional blockage that may be keeping us from our place of inner equilibrium and emotional stability.

Citrine breathes positivity, abundance and self-confidence into the Solar Plexus Chakra, balancing and aligning any self-doubt, darkness or depression with light, warmth and radiance.

Beneath this, Carnelian and Bloodstone at the Sacral and Root chakras respectively support physical and energetic vitality. Not only does this duo heal on a physical level, but they also encourage us to release toxic energy that may be throwing us out of alignment or causing imbalance within ourselves.

Both Carnelian and Bloodstone act as powerful detoxifiers, helping us to let go, release, recharge and reset energy that no longer serves us.

Hematite is an excellent balancing stone as it is naturally magnetic. When placed at the Earth Chakra, it effectively pulls all the imbalanced and non-serving energies earthwards and out of the body. Often, we can feel imbalanced if we are not adequately grounded in our daily lives, and Hematite is a wonderful stone for achieving grounding quickly.

Hematite at the Earth Chakra and Selenite at the Higher Crown Chakra work as gravitational opposites, pulling the energies towards themselves. This opens the space for energetic alignment to flow between them.

Blue Kyanite is one of the most powerful stones we can use for alignment, because its cellular arrangement is in a linear formation. In this vein, it naturally draws energy inwards and channels it up and down simultaneously.

By placing a piece of Kyanite between each of the chakras, we are strengthening both energetic poles, which allows energy to flow freely along the central meridian line of the body.

In addition, Kyanite brings a cleansing, calming energy and is an effective spine healer for those with back pain.

EXPERT TIPS

◊ Use a large wand or natural stick of Selenite or Blue Kyanite or a Lemurian Quartz wand to perform a simple spinal alignment. Point the crystal towards your partner and run it purposefully up and down the length of their body (along the chakra pathway) to draw the energies into alignment.

◊ Place Clear Quartz points (pointing inwards) round each main chakra crystal to amplify its energy and maximise this layout. You can also place double-terminated Quartz points in between each chakra if you are unable to source Kyanite blades.

CLARITY AND FOCUS

HEALING OUTCOMES

Clarity | Positive decision-making | Certainty | Better focus in work or study | Clearer perspective on situations | Productive planning and strategising

DIFFICULTY LEVEL

Intermediate

CRYSTAL PLACEMENT

EARTH:	Hematite
HIGHER CROWN:	Clear Quartz (upper) and Celestite (lower) (preferably clusters)
CROWN:	Clear Quartz
THIRD EYE:	Sodalite
HEART:	Emerald

CRYSTAL POINTS

» 2–4 Clear Quartz points placed around the top of the head, pointing in towards the head.

» 2–4 Amethyst points placed around the top of the head, pointing in towards the head.

» 2–6 Clear Quartz points placed around the Heart Chakra, pointing in towards the Emerald.

THE HEALING

Clear Quartz, Celestite and Sodalite are all stones for mental clarity, wisdom and calm. The better quality and clearer the Clear Quartz and Celestite, the stronger they will vibrate with 'clarity' energy.

Clear Quartz and Celestite work to cleanse anything that is clouding our vision and judgement. At the Crown and Higher Crown chakras, this clarity is drawn into our sphere of physical awareness. The Clear Quartz points further help to channel this energy in through the head.

Amethyst helps to enhance our intuition and wisdom for more intuitive and purposeful decision-making and thinking.

Sodalite at the Third Eye works by bringing calming, cleansing and focused energy to the Third Eye Chakra, while also assisting us in seeing the truth of a situation. It acts as a lens through which we can see with more clarity and eliminates 'brain fog' associated with indecisiveness and confusion.

It is important to acknowledge the Heart Chakra in this layout and to create a healthy connection between the head and the heart. Our emotional state heavily influences our cognitive processes so, to have clear vision in the mind, we need to have a clear and balanced emotional state. By using Emerald and Clear Quartz points at the Heart Chakra, we can help to achieve this outcome.

Emerald at the Heart Chakra energetically clears and releases emotional attachments that may be clouding our emotional or mental judgement.

We use Hematite specifically at the Earth Chakra in this layout to help bring confidence in decision-making. Hematite resonates with the mind and helps us to trust in ourselves, while anchoring and focusing our thoughts. It is also beneficial in releasing any self-doubt and uncertainty that may be blocking our clear path ahead.

EXPERT TIPS

◊ Invite your partner to visualise themselves staring at a dirty pane of glass, which they are cleaning. On the other side of the glass is the answer to their dilemma or a clear path forward. Ask them to imagine gradually cleaning the dirt from the glass and peering through to see the answers revealed on the other side.

◊ Relatively speaking, Hematite is an energetically heavy stone, so never place it above the Heart Chakra.

◊ For extra grounding and clarity in this layout, you can place an additional Hematite at the Sacral Chakra, which will help to integrate this focused energy into the Ego centre of the body, transforming it into determination.

TRANSITION AND CHANGE

HEALING OUTCOMES

Support during: Change of career | End of a relationship | New life path | Moving house | Change of circumstance | Natural life transition (such as menopause or puberty) | Crossroads in life

DIFFICULTY LEVEL

Intermediate

CRYSTAL PLACEMENT

EARTH:	Grounding stone of choice (Hematite, Obsidian, for example)
HIGHER CROWN:	Higher stone of choice (Selenite, Clear Quartz, for example)
THIRD EYE:	Labradorite
HEART:	Labradorite
SOLAR PLEXUS:	Citrine
SACRAL:	Chiastolite
ROOT:	Chiastolite

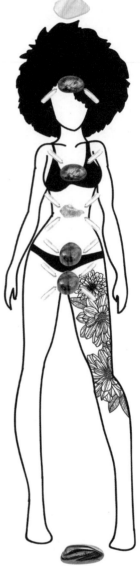

CRYSTAL POINTS

» 10–20 Clear Quartz points placed around the Third Eye, Heart, Solar Plexus, Sacral and Root chakras, pointing in towards the chakra stones.

THE HEALING

This crystal layout draws together the different spiritual natures of change. It helps minimise the effect that life's transitions have on our energetic and emotional bodies, while helping us to deal with the practical challenges that change brings.

Labradorite is a deeply mystical stone, used for deriving wisdom from situations that are usually beyond our realm of understanding. It calms the mind and stimulates the Third Eye and Heart chakras, bringing emotional insight and balance at times of turmoil. This insight helps us to 'see through' a situation and grasp the learning opportunity in what may otherwise be a confusing and upsetting experience.

Citrine at the Solar Plexus Chakra strengthens our ability to remain positive and inspired when things don't go to plan. Its sunny and positive energy can be channelled into the Solar Plexus to replace feelings of self-doubt with creativity, inspiration, optimism and confidence. This ability to 'spin straw into gold' is vital in breaking negative life-patterns and being able to move forward with even more power and strength than before.

Chiastolite is an interesting and unique stone. While it's not one of the prettier minerals, it certainly holds some powerful healing energy! The black 'cross' lines that dissect its brown surface represent the metaphorical crossroads that we all find ourselves facing at certain times in our lives.

Chiastolite brings grounding, decisive direction and focus. It also provides a solid reference point for us to mark and navigate from, helping us to make tough decisions and ground the emotions at times when they may become overwhelming.

Clear Quartz points placed around each of the chakras amplify and direct the energy flow of the crystals, bringing healing and cleansing on all levels.

EXPERT TIPS

◊   A guided visualisation that focuses on the concept of transformation (such as a caterpillar transforming into a butterfly or a snake shedding its skin) can complement this layout beautifully.

◊   You may also like to create a guided visualisation that involves approaching a crossroads on a long road with different navigational signposts for where to go next. This can be helpful in situations where a decision must be made and the potential outcomes need to be explored.

◊   Chiastolite, although a grounding stone, is safe to use on all chakras. However, always ensure its Earth-bound energy is balanced with a high-vibrational light stone (such as Amethyst or Clear Quartz) when working on the higher chakras. Without the support of an energetically lighter stone, Chiastolite can feel heavy and uncomfortable and may result in your partner feeling drained or flat afterwards.

COMMUNICATION AND PUBLIC SPEAKING

HEALING OUTCOMES

Clear communication | Speaking our truth | Voicing our opinion with conviction | Support for stuttering or mumbling | Confidence for singing and public speaking | Freedom of personal expression

DIFFICULTY LEVEL

Intermediate

CRYSTAL PLACEMENT

EARTH:	Black Obsidian
HIGHER CROWN:	Clear Quartz
THIRD EYE:	Sodalite
THROAT:	Blue Lace Agate (upper) and Citrine (lower)
SOLAR PLEXUS:	Tiger's Eye

CRYSTAL POINTS

» 2–4 Amethyst points placed around the Third Eye, pointing in towards the Sodalite crystal.

» 3 large Blue Kyanite blades placed just below and either side of the Citrine crystal. Two of the blades should point in towards the Throat Chakra like an arrowhead, with the tip of the arrowhead being the Citrine crystal. The third blade should be directly below the Citrine crystal, like the shaft of the arrow.

» 2 Clear Quartz points placed either side of the shaft Kyanite blade, also pointing upwards and in towards the Citrine crystal.

» 2–4 Citrine points placed around the Solar Plexus, pointing in towards the Tiger's Eye.

THE HEALING

This crystal layout will help to open the Throat Chakra and is excellent for healing all areas of communication and personal expression. It is especially beneficial if the chakra is in a weakened state.

The Throat Chakra resonates with the vibration of blue energy, so we use lots of beautiful blue stones on and around the throat area for this layout.

Sodalite, Kyanite and Blue Lace Agate are all stones for communication, honesty, strength of voice and personal expression. They help us find our inner truth and externalise this through integrity of expression. If we suppress our opinions and expression over a length of time, then the Throat Chakra can become blocked (or weakened) and throat illnesses can occur. We might begin to doubt our own voice and become fearful of speaking in the presence of others.

Sodalite is an amazing Throat Chakra healer, which can be used directly over the Throat Chakra to support communication. Its deep blue colour also resonates with the Third Eye Chakra and I have chosen to place it on the Third Eye in this layout, as its powers of communication, truth, calmness and clarity will be absorbed into this energy centre for developing intuition, wisdom and spiritual growth. Before we can speak with clarity and confidence, we must first embody these qualities on a deeper level, and Sodalite will help us with this process.

Blue Lace Agate on the Throat Chakra works to gently strengthen and heal this entire area. It is supported by Citrine, which is normally a stone for the Solar Plexus and Sacral chakras, but used here it brings radiant light energy and confidence to the Throat. This is essential to help illuminate any buried trauma associated with public speaking or personal expression, which can then be released.

The Throat Chakra is further supported by Kyanite, a high-vibrational stone. It helps us to understand truth on a deeper, more mystical level.

Kyanite assists us in finding words of wisdom. It helps us reach a spiritual understanding of what may be holding us back from expressing ourselves fully. Not only does it help to facilitate the communication process through voice, but it also clarifies our message and vision, so that we can communicate with more connection to our audience.

These energies are enhanced and supported by Amethyst points at the Third Eye and Clear Quartz at the Higher Crown.

The addition of these higher vibrational crystals is important, as we can begin to align our voice and expression with our higher purpose and speak words from a place of love, connection, wisdom and true clarity.

Confident speaking usually requires that we have a healthy sense of self-esteem. It's difficult to express ourselves authentically and confidently if we have low self-esteem and consider ourselves to be unworthy or insignificant. This makes it necessary to give the Solar Plexus Chakra some love and support in this layout also.

Powerful Tiger's Eye and Citrine work together to deliver light, inspiration and confidence through the Solar Plexus Chakra. Their powerful strength also helps to awaken our desire for achievement and success.

Finally, it is important to use Black Obsidian at the Earth Chakra in this layout, as it is highly successful in helping us release our deepest fears and insecurities.

By placing it at the Earth Chakra, it sits within the energetic part of us most closely related to our past and earthly foundations. Here, buried energetic trauma from our history can be acknowledged and processed, so that it no longer affects our present.

EXPERT TIPS

◊   Your partner may feel the need to cough during or after this session. Encourage this, as it will help with the clearing of the Throat Chakra.

◊   Performing some voice exercises during this layout will aid the clearing of the Throat Chakra. Try asking your partner to take some deep breaths, then exhale with an audible long 'ahh' sound. You can also suggest reciting mantras vocally such as 'My voice is strong and I speak my truth with power'.

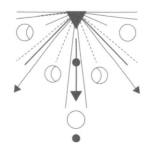

SEXUAL HEALTH

HEALING OUTCOMES

Increased sex-drive and desire | Better enjoyment of sex | Balanced masculine and feminine energies | Support for the reproductive organs | Support for male impotency

DIFFICULTY LEVEL

Intermediate

CRYSTAL PLACEMENT (MALE)

EARTH:	Grounding stone of choice (Hematite, Shungite, for example)
HIGHER CROWN:	Higher stone of choice (Clear Quartz, Selenite, for example)
SOLAR PLEXUS:	Citrine (upper) and Tiger's Eye (lower)
SACRAL:	Carnelian
ROOT:	Garnet (upper) and Shiva Lingam (lower)

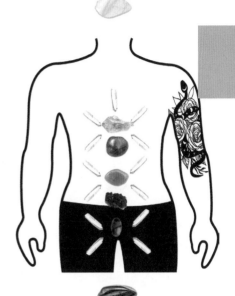

CRYSTAL PLACEMENT (FEMALE)

EARTH:	Grounding stone of choice (Hematite, Shungite, for example)
HIGHER CROWN:	Higher stone of choice (Clear Quartz, Selenite, for example)
HEART CHAKRA:	Rhodonite
SOLAR PLEXUS:	Citrine (upper) and Tiger's Eye (lower)
SACRAL:	Carnelian
WOMB:	Moonstone directly over the womb (uterus)
ROOT:	Garnet

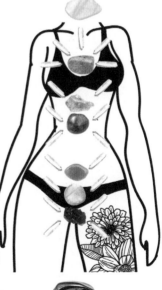

CRYSTAL POINTS (MALE AND FEMALE)

» 4–6 Clear Quartz points placed around each chakra point, pointing in towards the chakra.

THE HEALING

This layout varies slightly depending on whether you are working on a male or female partner.

MALE PARTNER

There can be many contributing factors when considering what may be causing low libido or sexual dysfunction in men. This may include (but is not limited to) age, testosterone levels, sexual history and psychological factors.

In this layout, we try to address some of these possible root causes by working on the Solar Plexus Chakra to establish self-confidence and balance, and the lower chakras for energetically supporting the sexual organs and releasing trauma (which may be impacting on your partner's sexual performance).

Citrine is a stone for inspiration, positivity, joy and abundance. At the Solar Plexus Chakra, it works to release any dark and depressing energies that may be weighing down our sense of self-confidence or limiting our achievement in life. When applied

to sexual dysfunction specifically, Citrine can help us overcome low self-confidence, lack of self-worth, shyness and performance anxiety.

This is supported by Tiger's Eye, which contains both earthly and astral energies, and is excellent for balancing energetic dualities within the Self. This includes harmonising and aligning the male and female energies that exist within each of us.

In order to have a healthy sexual relationship with ourselves or with another, these energies must be balanced in a way that is agreeable to all parties. For a very 'manly' man, this may mean attuning to his own feminine side or connecting more deeply to the feminine energies of his partner. For a more 'feminine' man, this may include stepping more into his alpha-male energy. Whatever the imbalance may be, Tiger's Eye will help to bring awareness and balance to this duality for a more harmonious relationship between the two.

Tiger's Eye is also excellent for physical and psychological protection, which can help reassure those who feel vulnerable during sexual activity. It can also assist in strengthening self-confidence.

Carnelian and Garnet work at the Sacral and Root chakras respectively to energetically heal and balance any disorder in the reproductive organs.

By clearing blockage through this area, we can release energetic trauma that may have accumulated as a result of injury, abuse or illness. Once this trauma has been released, we are much more likely to be able to experience enjoyable and prolonged sexual performance.

Carnelian and Garnet are both stones that assist in promoting stamina, stimulating kundalini energy and awakening sexual desire. Their potent energy warms the lower body and flows upwards, connecting with the Solar Plexus and Heart chakras for a more connected and fulfilling sexual experience.

Shiva Lingam is a unique stone, found and revered in India. Shiva is one of the most worshipped gods in Hinduism, and the word 'lingam' refers to the phallus (penis). Shiva Lingam stones represent Divine Masculine energy, and embody strength, virility and generative power.

When placed on the Root Chakra, these energies are absorbed into the auric field and are highly beneficial when working with male clients. Shiva Lingam can also be used on women who may need support in connecting with their masculine power.

FEMALE PARTNER

There can be many contributing factors when considering what may be causing low libido or sexual dysfunction in women, including (but not limited to) age, hormone levels, menopause, sexual and childbirth history, sexual abuse and psychological factors.

This layout is almost identical to the one outlined above; however, instead of using Shiva Lingam at the Root Chakra, we use Moonstone over the womb and add Rhodonite at the Heart Chakra.

At the risk of over-simplifying and generalising what is a complex and personal emotional journey, it is important to understand the differences between the male and female sexual experience. Women tend to be more emotionally engaged with their sexual experiences than men. This is not to say that men are not emotionally engaged; they absolutely can be! However, women more often seek emotional connection *before* initiating sexual intercourse, whereas men often use sexual intercourse as a *gateway* to establishing emotional connection with their partner.

The Heart Chakra can almost be considered the doorway to a woman's sexual world and can even be regarded as the first point for sexual foreplay. For this reason, it is essential that we honour the Heart Chakra during this layout, when working on a female partner. My stone of choice is the supportive and loving Rhodonite.

Rhodonite, while opening and strengthening the Heart Chakra, is also excellent for healing and releasing emotional pain, trauma and tension in this area. This in turn provides the perfect foundations for love to be laid at her doorstep and physical closeness to follow.

Moonstone is a powerful fertility stone, as it contains the energies of the moon and its cycles. This mirrors the natural monthly fertility cycles in women. Whether or not your partner is trying to fall pregnant, Moonstone speaks to her reproductive organs, softening and ripening the womb, so she is open and willing to receive her partner emotionally and sexually.

We use Clear Quartz points to amplify and strengthen this layout, connecting the chakras and helping the energies to flow freely throughout.

EXPERT TIPS

◊ Place your flat hands (palms facing down) just above your partner's pubic bone. Visualise sending warm, tingly, red healing energy into their body. Remember, if you are working in a professional setting, always be respectful and professional with your touch. Communicate with your client prior to the session about what they can expect and always ensure your client is safe and honoured during the healing.

◊ This can be a sensual and romantic layout to perform with a lover. Set the scene with candles and oils, and ask your lover to remove all their clothing. Perhaps start with a sensual oil massage before placing the crystals on their body. Once the crystals are in place, you can continue massaging their body or experiment with warm touch. You can even use the crystals as a massage tool and rub them gently over your lover's skin. Not only does this ritual develop intimacy and trust, but it is also physically and energetically stimulating.

◊ To take this layout to the next level with yourself or a lover, try introducing the use of a love-wand for internal stimulation and pleasure. Choose a wand made of Rose Quartz for a more loving, gentle experience; Red Jasper or Carnelian for a more erotic, stimulating experience; or Amethyst to encourage a more spiritually connected experience.

ABUNDANCE

HEALING OUTCOMES

Attracting financial wealth | Encouraging career success | Maximising your potential | Support when starting a new business venture | Release of a scarcity mindset | Identification and release of success blockers | Creating a positive relationship with wealth and success

DIFFICULTY LEVEL

Intermediate

CRYSTAL PLACEMENT

EARTH:	Grounding stone of choice (Hematite, Obsidian, for example)
HIGHER CROWN:	Amethyst
CROWN:	Blue Kyanite blade (vertical alignment)
THIRD EYE:	Blue Kyanite blade (vertical alignment)
THROAT:	Lapis Lazuli
HIGHER HEART:	Moldavite placed just above the Heart Chakra
HEART:	Chrysoprase
SOLAR PLEXUS:	Tiger's Eye
SACRAL:	Pyrite
ROOT:	Bloodstone

CRYSTAL POINTS

» 4 Citrine points placed around the Heart, Solar Plexus and Sacral chakras, pointing in towards each chakra.

» 2–4 Clear Quartz points placed around the head and the Heart, Solar Plexus and Sacral chakras, pointing inwards.

» A single Clear Quartz point placed between each chakra, pointing down towards the Root Chakra.

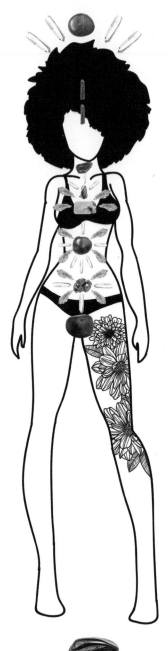

THE HEALING

It is vital to understand that energy healing works on the highest vibrational plane. This means it is simply impossible to use crystals for personal gain if your intentions are not pure or come from a low-vibrational place, such as ingratitude or greed. Whenever we perform a ritual or healing to attract wealth and abundance, we must be sure to frame it in a positive context; our intention should come from the highest place within ourselves.

The golden rule for manifesting abundance and reprogramming a scarcity mindset is to shift our energetic state to one of gratitude. Rather than focusing on what we lack (or our desperation for success), it is important to set our intention on growing what we already have. We do this by truly appreciating and feeling gratitude for our current life and state of abundance.

By applying our energy to maximising our natural skills and offerings with integrity, respect and good intention, we create a vibrational state that is matched by the universe. Opportunities will begin to present themselves. Unexpected windfalls will start rolling in.

Therefore, the purpose of this layout is not to magically manifest a pot of gold out of thin air. Rather, it is to help change your vibrational state to one more aligned with the universal flow of abundance and success. In this way, you can begin generating your own success and abundance, creating the life of your dreams!

Amethyst at the Higher Crown Chakra helps to purify our mental state so that we receive unpolluted wisdom. It acts as a 'messenger filter', ensuring that the Divine messages we receive through the Higher Crown Chakra do not become diluted or manipulated by our low-vibrational mental projections. It helps keep our intentions intact, so that we can clearly be guided towards our *dharma* (life purpose). Once we truly accept our dharma, we can manifest this into physical form and return it back into the world.

Abundance loves integrity. If you focus on what gifts you can share with the world (instead of what you can take from the world), abundance will be sure to follow.

To further support this process, Kyanite is used at the Third Eye and Crown chakras, working to bring truth and clarity to our vision for success, while helping us to maintain integrity and alignment with our personal value system.

Lapis Lazuli carries this energy into the Throat Chakra. It encourages us to voice our truth clearly and from a place of higher consciousness, while honouring ourselves and our place in the world with respect and gratitude.

At the Heart and Solar Plexus chakras, we have Chrysoprase and Tiger's Eye respectively. Chrysoprase is often used to attract prosperity in love and life, while Tiger's Eye protects against those who wish us misfortune, in addition to being known as a stone for attracting wealth.

This abundance energy is amplified by the surrounding Citrine and Clear Quartz points. As a stone of light, joy and cleansing, Citrine also gifts us with the positive mindset and confidence we need to pursue our path of success.

By placing Moldavite above the Heart Chakra, we are channelling the speeding energies of meteorites (from which Moldavite is derived). This stone is an essential addition to any manifestation work, because it expedites the realisation of our heart's desires. It helps us to work quickly and purposefully with our talents for the fastest path to success.

Pyrite (also known as Fools Gold) is a discerning stone. Used with integrity and without greed, it can multiply our wealth exponentially. However, just as its alternative name suggests, it can leave us empty-handed if our motives are not pure.

At the Sacral Chakra specifically, Pyrite can permeate our Ego layers, empowering us with the strength and determination to achieve our greatest level of success.

By working with a combination of Bloodstone at the Root Chakra and Clear Quartz points along the central meridian of the body, we can cleanse and release any blocked energy that is sabotaging our path to success. This may include self-doubt, low self-esteem, trauma from previous 'failures', non-serving beliefs, a scarcity mindset and so on. Once these are released and shed through the Root Chakra, the path to success is clear ahead!

EXPERT TIPS

◊   Encourage your partner to go home and create an 'abundance altar' to reflect on and manifest at daily. Incorporate abundance-attracting crystals, items of value, items that represent abundance and joy (such as happy family photos), and any other meaningful items that symbolise abundance and joy to them.

◊   Generate some positive visualisations and feelings of gratitude. Ask your partner to spend 10 minutes making a list of everything in their life they are grateful for. Invite them to sit with this list until they not only acknowledge their gratitude mentally, but feel the gratitude at their deepest core. You may even like to invite your partner to keep a daily gratitude journal.

◊   It can be difficult to break through and reprogram a 'victim' or 'poverty' mindset. One of the best ways to do this is by gifting to others less fortunate than ourselves. Giving to those who have less than we do reminds us that concepts around 'wealth' are entirely subjective. The idea of being 'poor' is only made real and meaningful by the feelings we attach to it. For example, a millionaire who loses his fortune and moves from a 10-bedroom mansion to a 3-bedroom house might consider himself to be poor. On the other hand, a person who has been homeless but now finds himself living in the same 3-bedroom house may now believe himself to be incredibly wealthy. Two different experiences, two different mindsets. Poverty, scarcity and lack are fluid concepts, which are completely shaped by each person's unique life experience and expectation. When we are in a slump, it is easy to believe that being 'disadvantaged' is our inescapable reality. However, this is simply our perception of our own situation and does not represent a cosmic truth. By allowing ourselves to become attached to this belief, we are only perpetuating our own (perceived) life of financial lack. By giving to others who are less fortunate than ourselves, we are reminded that wealth and money are purely conceptual. We can always find wealth and abundance in our own lives if we shift the spotlight from what we don't have to shine on everything that we do.

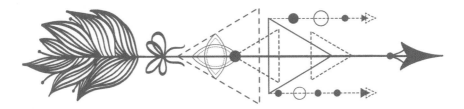

RESOLVING THE PAST

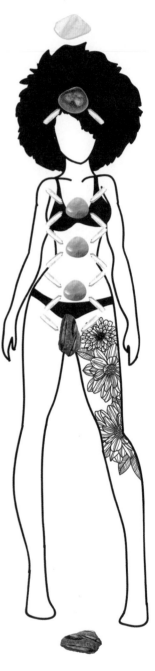

HEALING OUTCOMES

Release of energetic trauma associated with a past event | Healing old emotional wounds | Fostering forgiveness | Understanding, accepting and learning from past events | Releasing the control the past has over the present | Exploration and resolution of past lives | Healing support for childhood abuse | Understanding of how the past has shaped the present

DIFFICULTY LEVEL

Intermediate

CRYSTAL PLACEMENT

EARTH:	Grounding stone of choice (Orthoceras is a good choice for this layout)
HIGHER CROWN:	Clear Quartz
THIRD EYE:	Azurite
HEART:	Rose Quartz
SOLAR PLEXUS:	Rose Quartz
SACRAL:	Rose Quartz
ROOT:	Orthoceras

CRYSTAL POINTS

» 2–8 Clear Quartz points placed around each of the chakras, pointing in towards the main chakra stones.

THE HEALING

In this layout, we approach healing from three core aspects: intuitive, emotional and physical.

Azurite at the Third Eye Chakra works to connect us to our intuitive wisdom and understanding. It is well regarded as a stone for past life regression and is effective in bringing insight and understanding to events that have shaped our past.

Although these events and memories may be painful, Azurite helps to cast them into our sphere of awareness through the Third Eye, so that we can bear witness to them. From this perspective, we can observe the experiences that have shaped us in a way that shifts consciousness from lower dimensional judgement and pain to higher dimensional wisdom and understanding.

Rose Quartz is a gentle but beneficial healer. It is a major player in this layout, or any layout that may involve digging up old trauma and pain, because it provides emotional support as we process challenging experiences. It helps us to transform negative emotions such as judgement and hatred into higher vibrational states such as acceptance and love.

At the Heart Chakra, Rose Quartz works to support the emotions and open the heart to giving and receiving love in giant proportions. It gently permeates the emotional layers of the heart-space, encouraging us to find forgiveness, understanding and acceptance at times when these feelings may be lost to us.

Not only does Rose Quartz help us to forgive the actions of others, but, perhaps even more importantly, it helps us to forgive ourselves.

At the Solar Plexus Chakra, Rose Quartz softly reminds us of our inner strength and ability to love. Its gentle energy can assist us in transmuting pain and trauma into fuel for growth and inspiration.

At the Sacral Chakra, it can help us to identify old physical and emotional pain, then release it with love, so it no longer controls us.

Orthoceras is an amazing yet under-appreciated healer, which we introduced in the earlier 'Back pain' layout (see page 129). Because it is a fossil of a previously living organism, energetically speaking it acts as a time link for us to connect with the furthest reaches of our human evolution. For this reason, it is excellent for facilitating the exploration of a past time period, including childhood, previous generations and even past lives.

At the Root Chakra, Orthoceras works at an energetic level to bring forward any trauma in our past for healing, as well as providing grounding and support. It can be used to stabilise the emotions as we explore painful memories, while assisting us to process and accept events that we cannot change.

Given the fact that it was once a living being, Orthoceras reminds us that with death new birth can occur, as we transition through one state into another. 'Death' can come in many forms and is simply the end of one state before it transforms into another. Through its preserved existence, we are energetically reminded that it is okay to let go and lay the past to rest, because we have the power to transform even the most painful of experiences.

The Clear Quartz points throughout the layout help us to cleanse, release and heal, while channelling energy more purposefully throughout the grid.

EXPERT TIPS

◊ Any focused work on the Heart and Solar Plexus chakras can be very emotional. Always have tissues on hand and provide as much support as possible to your partner during and after the session. Invite your partner to do some journal writing or have a relaxing bath afterwards.

◊ I like to involve a lot of touch when working on the Heart and Solar Plexus chakras. I do this by placing my hands gently over the chakras and applying Reiki. You can simply place your hands (palms facing down) over your partner's Heart and Solar Plexus chakras. Close your eyes and focus on sending your love and healing energy into these energy centres.

◊ It may be helpful for your partner to perform a 'letting go' ritual at some point soon after the session. There are many ways we can let go of the past. Some suggestions include:

» Write important names, feelings, events or other situations of significance on pieces of paper, then burn them in a candle flame. Visualise the smoke carrying the painful memories away.

» Bury symbolic items from your past and sprinkle the soil with seeds. Water and care for the seeds until they sprout; this represents caring for yourself. Eventually, the plants will grow and produce beautiful flowers or fruits, which symbolises the journey of transformation from pain to growth and your ultimate 'blossoming'.

» Create a sand and shell mandala or sculpture at the beach to represent your past trauma. Reflect over it and stay with it until the waves wash it away. Feel the release that comes with watching this creation being dissolved by the cleansing water.

CLAIRVOYANCE AND DREAMS

HEALING OUTCOMES

Enhancing or awakening clairvoyant ability | Support for psychic development | Improving the visionary quality of dreams | Developing a stronger connection to the unconscious mind | Deeper meditation experience | Enhancing or awakening visionary ability

DIFFICULTY LEVEL

Intermediate

CRYSTAL PLACEMENT

EARTH:	Grounding stone of choice (Hematite, Smoky Quartz, for example)
HIGHER CROWN:	Moonstone
CROWN:	Amethyst
THIRD EYE:	Lapis Lazuli (or Iolite)
HIGHER HEART:	Chrysocolla
HEART:	Lepidolite (pink or purple)
ROOT:	Hematite

CRYSTAL POINTS

» 2–4 Amethyst points placed around the top of the head, pointing down towards the head.

» 2–4 Clear Quartz points placed around the top of the head, pointing down towards the head.

» 2–4 Clear Quartz points placed around the Heart Chakra, pointing in towards the heart, and one below the Heart Chakra, pointing down to the Root Chakra.

» 2–4 Clear Quartz points placed around the top of the Root Chakra, pointing down towards the Root Chakra as though directing energy flow out of the body.

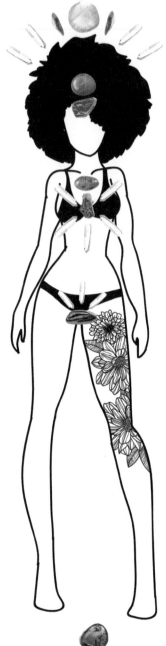

THE HEALING

This layout includes some potent visionary stones. While each stone is individually mystical, in this concentrated combination the stones work together to provide a truly spiritual and transcendent experience.

Amethyst, Clear Quartz, Moonstone and Lapis Lazuli (or Iolite) all work together on the higher plane to stimulate the Third Eye and Crown chakras.

High-vibrational Moonstone naturally resonates with the moon and lunar energies. It carries us gently into the cosmic night-time realms and provides a guiding light to us at times of darkness and sleep. It calms the mind and relaxes our earthly psychic boundaries by communicating with us during our sleep-state consciousness.

Once the doorway to this level of consciousness has been opened, Amethyst, Lapis Lazuli and Clear Quartz can then gently enter, expanding our psychic and visionary abilities.

Clear Quartz brings clarity to our vision, while Lapis Lazuli brings truth and understanding to our experience. Together, they form a cohesive energetic 'window' that allows us to peer into the higher realms to seek knowledge that otherwise may have been invisible to us.

Above the heart at the Higher Heart Chakra, Chrysocolla, which is famed for its relaxing and peaceful qualities, calms and settles the emotions. This allows us to relax and shift into a more surrendered emotional state, allowing a stream of consciousness to flow through us, unhindered by emotional attachment.

Chrysocolla also provides psychic and emotional protection, as we explore the higher vibrational realms.

At the Heart Chakra, Lepidolite brings emotional balance. It is a wonderful stress-reliever and can improve dream recollection, as well as enhancing the visionary depth of our dreams. It is especially effective in helping us to understand the messages we receive through our dreams and in altered states. This makes it a crystal of choice among clairvoyants and soul searchers.

Hematite at the Root Chakra helps us remain anchored. It provides an exit point for any unwanted stress and tension that prevents us from reaching the deepest sleep-state. It also helps keep us grounded and earthed during advanced visionary experiences, which is vital when working on such a high-vibrational level.

Clear Quartz points amplify and direct the energy flow, bringing healing and cleansing on all levels.

EXPERT TIPS

◊   Invite your partner to place one or more of the stones from this layout under their pillow for a dream-filled sleep.

◊   I recommend using a sweat band to hold crystals against the Third Eye Chakra while you sleep. This is a great way of receiving the full benefit of the stones while you are in an altered and surrendered state of consciousness.

◊   If your partner is in a heightened state already, it is advisable to use additional grounding stones at the Earth Chakra. Place one at each heel, plus one between the ankles to provide extra grounding for those who need it. Choose strong grounding stones such as Hematite, Shungite, Black Tourmaline or Black Obsidian.

HAPPINESS AND JOY

HEALING OUTCOMES

More joy and positivity | Improved mindset and mood |
Releasing negative thought patterns | Emotional support
for 'flat' or 'blue' days

DIFFICULTY LEVEL

Intermediate

CRYSTAL PLACEMENT

EARTH:	Black Tourmaline
HIGHER CROWN:	Clear Quartz
CROWN:	Citrine
THIRD EYE:	Rainbow Quartz
HEART:	Rose Quartz
SOLAR PLEXUS:	Citrine
SACRAL:	Sunstone

CRYSTAL POINTS

» 4–8 Amethyst points placed around the top of the head and
the Solar Plexus Chakra, pointing inwards.

» 4–8 Citrine points placed around the top of the head and the
Heart, Solar Plexus and Sacral chakras, pointing inwards.

THE HEALING

There are few stones in the crystal kingdom that embody
the qualities of happiness and light as beautifully as a
rainbow crystal. Crystals that contain rainbows are quite
special. Natural rainbows can only occur when there has
been an internal cracking or imperfection in the crystal
that creates a prism-like effect. The shards and multiple

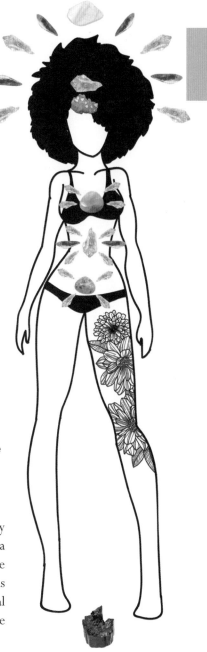

faces of the imperfection catch the light as it enters the crystal, creating beautiful rainbows when the crystal is held at certain angles.

Energetically, these crystals are full of positivity and joy, because the crystal has absorbed damage and imperfection, only to transmute it into something magnificent. This is a defining quality in individuals who somehow always seem to be able to turn a challenging situation into something positive.

Applied to the purpose of this layout, rainbow crystals offer a powerful energetic influence on the human psyche.

Rainbows are naturally found among the more transparent crystals, such as Clear Quartz, Smoky Quartz, Clear Calcite and Amethyst. They are not to be confused with artificially created iridescent stones, such as Aura Quartz. If you are fortunate, you may even find a Citrine crystal that contains rainbows! Citrine is already a powerful stone when it comes to channelling positive energy, so to find one with rainbows is a rare treasure.

In this layout, we support our partner psychologically with Clear Quartz, Citrine and Amethyst at the Higher Crown. These stones all hold and amplify pure light energy. They introduce warmth, light and illumination into our auric field, chasing away any darkness that may be shadowing our souls.

Clear Quartz works to heal and cleanse on the highest energetic level, bringing clarity to our vision. It connects us to our Highest Self and encourages us to transform a negative state of mind.

We place Citrine beneath the Clear Quartz, because its energies of positivity, inspiration and joy are swept up in the flow that enters our body through the Higher Crown Chakra. This effectively flushes away and lifts heaviness and negativity out of the mind, which may be weighing us down psychologically.

Amethyst is a true psychological healer, instilling feelings of inner peace and serenity, while strengthening connection to Spirit. At the Crown Chakra, the Amethyst points help us expand our view of a situation, so that we can approach life's challenges with more vision and understanding.

Joy and happiness are the high-vibrational opposites of energetically dense states, such as ingratitude and negativity. For this reason, we want to ensure this crystal layout is drawing the energies upwards, which makes Citrine an excellent choice for the Crown Chakra.

We place a Rainbow Quartz (or a similar rainbow crystal) at the Third Eye Chakra, so that the energy of positive transformation is absorbed directly by the psyche.

Rainbow crystals help us to see the bright side of any adverse situation, reminding us that joy and beauty can be found in the most difficult of circumstances. A rainbow crystal is a living example of how damage from a negative experience can be transformed into something dazzling.

At the Heart Chakra, Rose Quartz teaches us to love ourselves unconditionally and to navigate life's emotional rollercoaster with understanding and support. It is important to be at peace with ourselves and the world around us in order to feel joy on such a deep emotional level.

Sunstone at the Sacral Chakra resonates with positivity, radiance and joy. Like the sun, it shines warm light on this part of ourselves, helping us to overcome self-doubt, depression and negativity, and replacing these non-serving feelings with a sunnier disposition.

We use Black Tourmaline specifically in this layout at the Earth Chakra, because it not only provides grounding, but also shields us from outside negative influences that may be bringing us down. This crystal helps to clear and release negative thought patterns and can be effective in preventing dark energies from entering our energy field.

EXPERT TIPS

◊ Hold your hands, palms down, over your partner's Solar Plexus Chakra. Visualise the sun shining through the back of your hands and flowing into your partner through your palms. You will begin to feel heat as this energy flows through your hands and into your partner, flushing away any energy blockage.

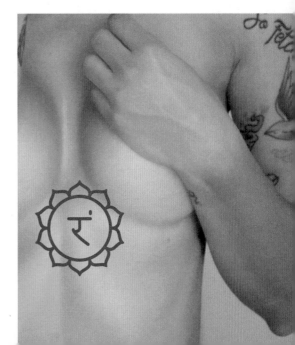

◊ Each thought we have has a measurable energetic vibration that shapes our belief system, our neurological system and, ultimately, our experience of life. We can speed up the effect of any external crystal or energetic treatment by also practising conscious reprogramming of our thoughts. To make lasting, long-term changes to negative thought patterns, it is important to practise conscious brain 'rewiring'. The first step is to acknowledge any non-serving thought patterns that we may have (such as 'I'm too fat', 'Nothing ever goes my way' or 'I can't afford it'). Then we can begin to make conscious changes and use more positive language in our self-talk (such as 'I have a curvaceous, healthy body', 'How can I make this situation work for me?' or 'I am abundant and have all that I need'). Over time, these positive thoughts will require less conscious effort and will become second nature!

HEALTH AND WELLNESS

HEALING OUTCOMES

Increased feeling of wellness | Feeling refreshed, balanced and cleansed | Healing support for mild illness and fatigue | Feeling nourished and nurtured | Support for all levels of wellbeing

DIFFICULTY LEVEL

Intermediate

CRYSTAL PLACEMENT

EARTH:	Black Tourmaline
HIGHER CROWN:	Clear Quartz
THIRD EYE:	Purple Fluorite
THROAT:	Blue Lace Agate
HEART:	Rose Quartz
SOLAR PLEXUS:	Chrysoprase
SACRAL:	Bloodstone
ROOT:	Smoky Quartz

CRYSTAL POINTS

» 2–4 Amethyst points placed around the Higher Crown Chakra, pointing down towards the head.

» 2–4 Clear Quartz points placed around the Heart Chakra, pointing inwards towards the heart.

» 3 large Citrine points placed below the Solar Plexus Chakra, pointing up and inwards, towards the chakra.

THE HEALING

This layout provides an all-round 'feel good' experience. It is designed to support health and wellness throughout the body's energy systems, and can be used any time on people of all ages and stages in life.

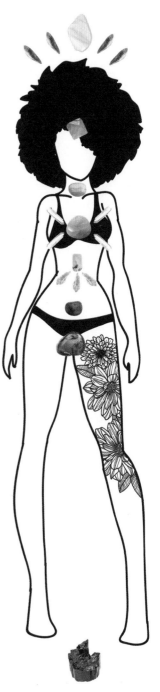

At the Higher Crown Chakra, Clear Quartz works to open the gateway between worlds. It cleanses and supports the brain, as well as expanding the consciousness, inviting healing on all levels.

Clear Quartz is supported either side by Amethyst and at the Third Eye Chakra by Purple Fluorite, both of which channel spiritual awareness and wisdom into the mind. This relaxing energy also calms busy thoughts, promoting a near-meditative state, so that we can experience deep, restorative sleep and peace within.

Blue Lace Agate is to the Throat Chakra what Rose Quartz is to the Heart Chakra. Gentle yet powerful, it works to energetically heal the entire Throat Chakra area. This includes relaxing tension in the shoulders and neck, calming the mind and clearing the way for us to communicate and express ourselves more clearly.

Rose Quartz brings emotional comfort and healing to the Heart Chakra. It can help on a physical level to calm emotional anxiety and settle skin disorders. On the energetic level, it balances the heart and gently supports the emotional self.

Below this, Chrysoprase invites clarity and healing into the body. It helps us to tap into our inner well of resources, so that we can manifest health and prosperity.

Citrine points amplify the properties of the other stones in the layout and fill the Solar Plexus Chakra with radiance and vitality. It can reduce depression and winter-induced illness (such as flu and seasonal mood disorders), while replenishing the Solar Plexus with positivity, creativity and health.

At the Sacral Chakra, Bloodstone works to cleanse the body of physical and energetic waste such as toxins, illness and lethargy, drawing the toxicity downwards. It also helps cleanse the lower digestive system and sexual organs.

Smoky Quartz at the Root Chakra captures the dislodged energy from the Solar Plexus and redirects it out of the body for elimination.

In addition to the benefits that each stone brings to individual chakras, Smoky Quartz, Bloodstone, Clear Quartz and Chrysoprase work harmoniously to protect from environmental pollution. Their unique cellular structure means they are capable of absorbing and filtering harmful electromagnetic frequencies (such as microwave emissions), which are thought to have negative health implications.

At the Earth Chakra, Black Tourmaline provides stability, grounding, focus, concentration, clarity and mental sharpness. It also helps the high-vibrational healing to be absorbed and integrated into the physical plane for whole-body harmony and alignment.

EXPERT TIPS

◊ Follow this session with an aura-smudge. To do this, light a tiny amount of white sage (or another sacred herb) in a dish. Use your hand or a large feather to fan and waft the smoke around and through your partner's aura. Be sure to sweep away any heaviness or blockage weighing down their energy field. You may like to begin at your partner's head and sweep the smoke downwards towards the ground. Aura-smudging is a great way to quickly recharge yourself on a low-vibe day too!

◊ Make sure your partner drinks lots of water, and takes time for rest and recovery after receiving this healing. This assists in flushing out any toxins from the body and replenishes depleted energy stores.

◊ Create an even more nurturing experience for your partner by incorporating essential oils and massage into this treatment. Experiment with some gentle head and Third Eye massage, or a foot rub after the crystal work. Your partner will float out the door afterwards!

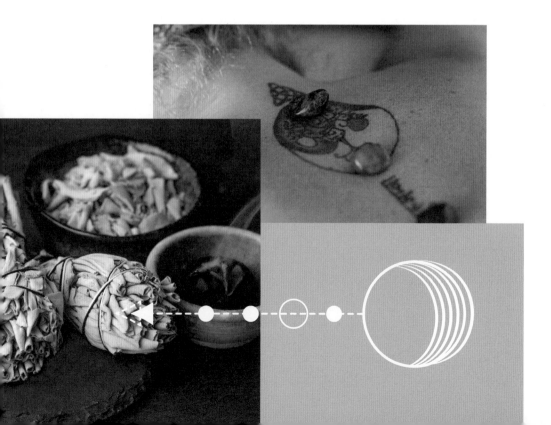

MENOPAUSE

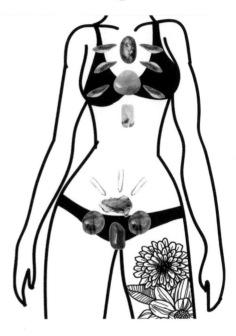

HEALING OUTCOMES

Relief for symptoms of menopause and hormonal imbalance | Healing support through menopause

DIFFICULTY LEVEL

Intermediate

CRYSTAL PLACEMENT

EARTH:	Grounding stone of choice (Hematite, Black Tourmaline, for example)
HIGHER CROWN:	Higher stone of choice (Selenite, Clear Quartz)
HIGHER HEART:	Labradorite
HEART:	Rose Quartz
SOLAR PLEXUS:	Chrysoprase
ABOVE ROOT:	Moldavite placed just above the Root Chakra
ROOT:	Red Jasper
OVARIES:	Chiastolite placed over each ovary

CRYSTAL POINTS

- » 4–8 Amethyst points placed around the Heart and Higher Heart chakras. Point the crystals towards the chakra but angle them slightly upwards.
- » 2–4 Clear Quartz points placed around the top of the Moldavite, pointing towards the Root Chakra.

THE HEALING

This layout is a great example of how we can use crystal healing to treat a specific physical area of the body, such as the female reproductive system.

Whenever we are targeting specific body areas for treatment, we do not have to limit ourselves to working only with the chakras. Instead, try to tailor the layout to the specific body part (or area of the body), taking into account the physical, symptomatic and energetic aspects of the ailment.

Women who are approaching or going through menopause may experience all or some of the following uncomfortable symptoms related to hormonal imbalance: mood swings, hot flushes, insomnia, heavier periods, irregular menstrual cycle, pain in the abdominal region, weight gain, emotional instability and more. In this layout, we attempt to address all these symptoms cohesively.

Menopause can be an emotional time for a woman, especially if she does not identify with the changes taking place in her body, which can lead to feelings of judgement and low self-esteem. That's why it is so important to provide support and healing to the Heart and Solar Plexus chakras.

By strengthening these energy centres with Chrysoprase and Rose Quartz, we can help to balance out the energies of emotional dysfunction and instability caused by hormonal imbalance.

Chrysoprase at the Solar Plexus Chakra helps to maintain emotional balance and health. Its soothing mint-green energy works to cool hot flushes and feelings of heat in the body. It acts like a wet blanket over a fire, quickly smothering any prickly hot emotions before they erupt. Chrysoprase also provides support and confidence during times when our self-esteem may be wavering.

At the Heart Chakra, Rose Quartz brings qualities of love, support and acceptance. This is beneficial if your partner is experiencing uncontrollable weight gain or changing body shape, as it reminds her to be gentle with herself.

Rose Quartz works together with the more intuitive and mystical qualities of Labradorite at the Higher Heart Chakra. Together, they bring emotional balance and understanding during this time of transformation.

Labradorite is infused with Divine Feminine energy and is therefore a gentle and wise companion through the different stages of womanhood. During menopause, it can help us to let go of the Maiden and Mother archetypes, and welcome and embrace the archetype of the Crone (or Wise Woman).

We use a combination of Moldavite, Chiastolite and Red Jasper directly over the reproductive organs, which all strategically work together on a more physical plane.

Chiastolite is a stone for transition and change. It helps us to navigate through the physical and hormonal changes of menopause with more understanding and respect for the process. It is solid and sure at those times when uncontrollable changes might threaten to destabilise us.

Red Jasper energetically heals and supports the reproductive organs, while Moldavite is a stone for speed and amplification. Sometimes menopause can be quite prolonged, so we include Moldavite in this layout to encourage a speedier transition process.

Moldavite can also be effective in amplifying the healing properties of all the other crystals in the layout.

The addition of Clear Quartz points at the lower chakras sends healing and cleansing energy into the reproductive organs. This can be beneficial for flushing out any blocked energy associated with menopause.

EXPERT TIPS

◊ It can be a beautiful experience for your partner to soak in a calming bath infused with rose essential oil and Rose Quartz after this session. This will help her to feel extra nourished and supported, while also continuing to support her emotionally. Adding Epsom salts and other crystals such as tumbled Labradorite or Clear Quartz helps facilitate a deeper cleanse and release. Always select smooth, tumbled stones (no sharp edges!) and non-porous stones if placing them in your bath water.

◊ Menopause is another of life's important transition stages that should be marked with ritual and respect. Encourage your partner to honour this process with a meaningful ritual that symbolises her own unique transformation. A women's circle to share experience with the female sisterhood is a beautiful way of doing this.

SPIRITUAL AWAKENING

HEALING OUTCOMES

Deepened sense of spiritual growth and ascension |
Opening of Crown and Third Eye chakras | Guidance during
an existential crisis | Heightened intuition and psychic
abilities | Exploration of our own spiritual potential

DIFFICULTY LEVEL

Intermediate

CRYSTAL PLACEMENT

EARTH:	Grounding stone of choice (Hematite, Black Tourmaline, for example)
HIGHER CROWN:	Selenite
CROWN:	Amethyst
THIRD EYE:	Sugilite (or Charoite)
HEART:	Labradorite (upper) and Rose Quartz (lower)
SOLAR PLEXUS:	Chiastolite
ROOT:	Hematite

CRYSTAL POINTS

» 12–20 Clear Quartz points placed around each of the
chakras with the points facing inwards. Place one Clear
Quartz point in between each chakra, pointing down
towards the Root Chakra.

THE HEALING

To gain the most effect from a high-vibe healing
experience, we must integrate it into the physical
body. This layout balances very high-dimensional
healing work with solid grounding and integration for the most transformative results.

As mentioned previously, Selenite is an incredibly high-vibration healer. At the Higher Crown Chakra, it connects us to the angelic realms and repels any low-vibrational energy from our aura. Its striated structure makes it excellent for bringing balance and alignment to all the chakras. This quality is especially beneficial during the significant energetic shifts that come with spiritual ascension work, which can leave us feeling energetically off-balance. Selenite helps to bring us back to centre.

Amethyst at the Crown Chakra works to channel and enhance intuition and spiritual vision. Its ascended energy draws in higher dimensional wisdom and understanding, as well as clearing away mental clutter from the brain. This spaciousness in the mind creates the liberation we need to move forward psychologically towards our spiritual evolution.

Often, when we experience fast spiritual ascension, we can feel judgement or lose resonance with those around us who are not on the same path. For example, we may have a partner who does not share our spiritual vision. Rather than accept their unique journey with unconditional love, we may be tempted to resent them for not keeping up with our new growth process.

Sugilite at the Third Eye Chakra helps us to transcend any feelings of judgement towards others during this time. It resonates with the energy of universal love and encourages us to greet our new spiritual pathway with trust and acceptance. It also reminds us to channel some of this unconditional love to those who may not share our beliefs or spiritual direction.

In addition to bringing unconditional love, Sugilite can promote psychic vision, personal evolution and heightened awareness during times of intense spiritual awakening.

At the Heart Chakra, Mystical Labradorite helps us to better understand all that is going on in our sometimes confusing spiritual world. Its soothing energy calms the mind and brings wisdom on a mental, emotional and spiritual level.

Labradorite can also be valuable in gently guiding us through large life-transitions with grace and understanding.

Also at the Heart Chakra, Rose Quartz provides us with the emotional support we need at such a transformational time. It reminds us to approach our growth and transition with acceptance and to honour ourselves throughout the journey.

Sometimes we must face painful or difficult truths before we can evolve spiritually, so Rose Quartz ensures we remain emotionally supported through the different stages of our ascension.

Finally, with all this high-vibrational energy flowing through us, we need to anchor it into the physical body and ensure we remain grounded, so as not to become disconnected from our earthly existence.

Chiastolite provides excellent grounding, as well as clarity in navigating this new and exciting path. Its symbolic crossroads encourages certainty in our direction of growth and helps us choose the path that is most beneficial for our continued evolution.

Naturally magnetic Hematite furthers this transition process by drawing all the stagnant energy downwards and out of the body. By releasing energetic blockage, we are removing any unseen obstacles that may obstruct our spiritual growth.

The dense physical weight of Hematite also aids our physical body's absorption of all the high-vibrational healing energy from the crystals for a huge spiritual shift.

The Clear Quartz points amplify and direct the energy flow, bringing healing, support and cleansing on all levels.

EXPERT TIPS

◊ Because each spiritual journey is unique for each person, you may like to invite your partner to select a couple of crystals intuitively to hold during the healing session. This will help to provide them with exactly what they need at that moment to best support their ascension process.

◊ If your partner is finding the spiritual growth process a little unsettling, then some additional grounding activities can be stabilising. Encourage them to try gardening, barefoot beach walks, creating rock art, seated meditation, eating root vegetables and yoga to help create greater balance.

INNER PEACE

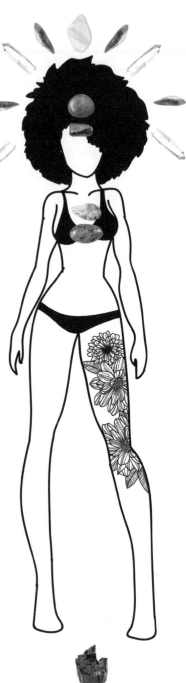

HEALING OUTCOMES

Increased feelings of calm, tranquillity and peace | Relief from mild stress | Release from mental clutter | Deeper meditation experience | Acceptance of things beyond our control

DIFFICULTY LEVEL

Intermediate

CRYSTAL PLACEMENT

EARTH:	Grounding stone of choice (Hematite, Black Tourmaline, for example)
HIGHER CROWN:	Clear Quartz
CROWN:	Amethyst
THIRD EYE:	Sodalite
HIGHER HEART:	Amazonite
HEART:	Chrysocolla

CRYSTAL POINTS

» 4–8 Amethyst points placed around the top of the head, pointing down towards the head.
» 4–8 Clear Quartz points placed around the top of the head, pointing away from the head.

THE HEALING

In this layout, we harness the deeply calming and spiritual nature of Amethyst through the higher chakras.

As a significant stone for the New Age, Amethyst is the hero crystal in this layout, which focuses on mindful connection, spiritual awareness, heightened intuition and developing a sense of inner peace and wisdom.

At the Higher Crown and Crown chakras, Clear Quartz and Amethyst act as an energetic conduit to channel energy from the spiritual realms into the physical body.

Clear Quartz points at the Crown Chakra and Sodalite at the Third Eye Chakra support this process by cleansing anything clouding our intuitive vision.

Furthermore, they work beautifully together to replace mental tension with a sense of calm and space. Once the mind is clear, it is better able to receive subtle messages from the spirit realm, so that the true meaning behind the message does not become lost or manipulated.

Clear Quartz points pointing outwards around the head provide a pathway for stressful thoughts to exit the mind. Through this mental cleansing process, psychological clutter, such as mental blocks and negative programming, is released, helping us to re-establish a state of mental equilibrium.

An imbalanced emotional state can wreak havoc on our mental health. If the heart is in turmoil, then it is tough for the mind to be calm, so this layout balances both the mental and emotional energies. By working in equilibrium, the head and heart can achieve a sense of true inner balance within ourselves.

Amazonite at the Higher Heart Chakra brings balance and stability to the emotions, while Chrysocolla (which has a reputation for being the stone of tranquillity) completely placates and protects the heart from unsettling feelings. We are then better able to free ourselves from any emotional blocks that may be preventing us from achieving a state of deep peace.

EXPERT TIPS

◊   To help create the most relaxing atmosphere possible during this healing session, try dimming the lights and diffusing some calming essential oils.

◊   If your partner usually finds it difficult to unwind and relax, then some extra attention can be given to helping them get settled. Take them through a guided relaxation prior to placing the crystals, encouraging them to disengage from any busy thoughts. Ask them to soften and let go of any stress, worry and tension they may be carrying in their mind or body, and perhaps apply soothing touch. A gentle head or Third Eye massage may help.

◊   A dab of lavender massage oil on the temples and forehead can help the relaxation process, while minimising the possibility of headache symptoms that may occur from working intensely on the higher chakras.

ENERGY

HEALING OUTCOMES

Increased energy | Increased motivation | Feeling more alert and 'awake' | Greater stamina and vitality

DIFFICULTY LEVEL

Intermediate

CRYSTAL PLACEMENT

EARTH:	Grounding stone of choice (Hematite, Black Tourmaline, for example)
HIGHER CROWN:	Higher stone of choice (Clear Quartz, Selenite, for example)
SOLAR PLEXUS:	Tiger's Iron
SACRAL:	Carnelian
ROOT:	Red Garnet

CRYSTAL POINTS

» 4–8 Citrine points placed around the Solar Plexus Chakra, pointing inwards and angled slightly upwards.

» 10–20 Clear Quartz points placed around each chakra with at least half of them angled upwards.

THE HEALING

Whenever we provide healing support for a condition in any area of the body, we need to consider the underlying causes in addition to addressing the symptoms themselves.

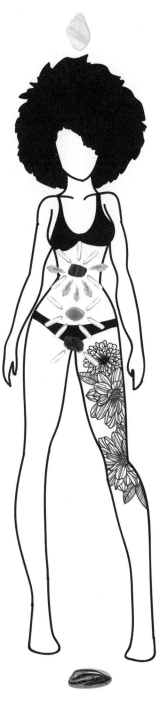

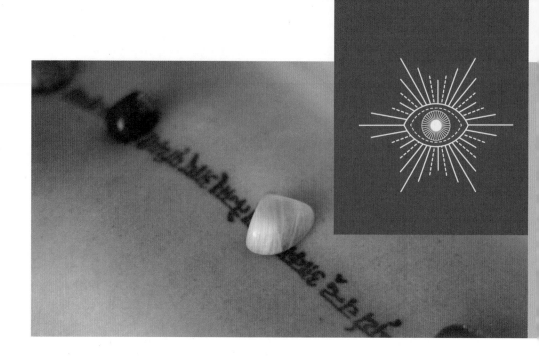

For a person who is regularly low in energy, we must consider what may be contributing to this lethargy. Lifestyle and health factors often play a huge role, so take this into account when deciding on the best crystal healing layout to use.

Some of the most common causes of energy loss include iron deficiency, sluggish digestive system, compromised immune system, sleep deprivation, poor nutrition, lack of motivation or self-worth, busy lifestyle and disconnection from our purpose. This layout aims to address most of these possible underlying causes.

Most of the stones in this layout cannot be substituted because of their unique properties, so please try to remain as true as possible to the crystals described.

Tiger's Iron is a unique combination of Hematite, Red Jasper and Tiger's Eye, which makes it a stone of choice for this layout specifically.

Hematite is an iron-rich mineral, which means it energetically resonates with and nourishes the blood. It can help the body to utilise iron more efficiently, while providing grounding and cleansing. This makes it perfect for those with low iron (or anaemia), while also helping to replenish and restore vitality on a physical level.

Red Jasper is a natural energy-booster used to cleanse and energise the lower chakras and stimulate kundalini energy.

Tiger's Eye brings motivation, energy and self-confidence. It also attracts abundance, which means it can motivate us to act on things that will bring us success and wealth.

When placed at the Solar Plexus Chakra and supported by Citrine, all the qualities of Tiger's Iron are delivered directly into our activity centre. This can trigger a sudden burst of inspiration to create, achieve and succeed, providing us with the motivation we need to act.

On an emotional and psychological level, Tiger's Iron helps us find the energy we need to 'face the day' and be productive.

Through the lower chakras, Carnelian and Red Garnet encourage healing on the physical and energetic planes. They work to purge a sluggish digestive system of blocked energy, which may be the result of food intolerance, inflammation, overeating, constipation, alcohol or too much meat or carbohydrate, any of which can drain our energy resources.

The simple process of digestion consumes a huge proportion of our body's energy reserves. There is a reason why we lose our appetites when we are unwell. This is the body's way of directing energy away from digestion and channelling it into more important body functions (such as fuelling the immune system) to fight illness.

Similarly, overeating or eating heavy foods can leave us feeling 'wiped out'. Think about how tired and lazy you can feel after eating a large bowl of pasta or a pizza!

Not only does Red Garnet energetically cleanse and support the digestive system, but also it replaces and amplifies our natural energy reserves, which are usually stored in the sacral area of the body. It enhances the libido by awakening and stimulating the Root Chakra, while regulating stamina and energy throughout the physical body.

We use lots of Clear Quartz points in this layout to provide a strong network of channels for energy to flow through. Clear Quartz is cleansing, healing and purifying, so the downward-facing points will help to flush out any energetic blockages that may be obstructing the flow of energy around the body.

Clear Quartz points that are angled upwards will help in raising energy levels by sending energy up the body towards the higher chakras.

EXPERT TIPS

◊ One of the best and most effective energy conductors in the natural world is copper. Copper is used in electrical wiring and batteries because it is so effective in carrying electrical currents. Crystals have a measurable energetic vibrational frequency, for which copper is just as an effective conduit. To advance this layout, place copper wire or pieces of raw copper around the main chakra crystals. The copper will carry and amplify vibrational energy throughout the aura, helping to thoroughly clear any energetic blockage. It will also help to recharge the body's natural energy stores.

◊ If you are unable to source a large, reasonably priced piece of Garnet for this layout, then you may substitute it with Red Jasper.

◊ It can be beneficial to support this layout with a metabolic fast, drawing energy away from digestion and reinvesting it into the energetic body. Encourage your partner to abstain from eating for at least two hours before and after the healing. You may also like to suggest they experiment with intermittent fasting as a way of giving their body the opportunity to rest and replenish. Please keep in mind that intermittent fasting is not advisable for anyone who has diabetes, who is pregnant or breastfeeding, who is still growing, or who has any other medical condition that may be negatively impacted by fasting.

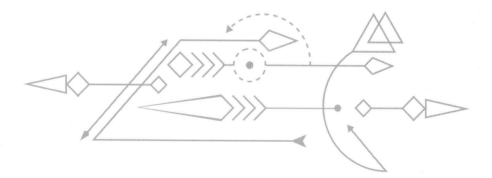

ANGER

HEALING OUTCOMES

Reduction in frequency or intensity of rage-based emotions | Increased patience and emotional stability | Reduced feelings of frustration | Improved relationships | Greater calm and emotional balance

DIFFICULTY LEVEL

Advanced

CRYSTAL PLACEMENT

EARTH:	Smoky Quartz
HIGHER CROWN:	Moonstone
CROWN:	Lepidolite
THIRD EYE:	Chrysocolla
THROAT:	Sodalite
HEART:	Emerald (or Green Aventurine)
SOLAR PLEXUS:	Chrysoprase
SACRAL:	Citrine
ROOT:	Hematite

CRYSTAL POINTS

» 2 Blue Kyanite blades placed just below and either side of the Throat Chakra, pointing in towards the Sodalite stone.

» 4–6 Citrine points placed around both the Heart and Solar Plexus chakras, pointing in towards each chakra.

» 4–6 Amethyst points placed around the top of the head, pointing down towards the head.

» 2 Clear Quartz points placed either side of the Sacral and Root chakras, pointing inwards and angled down towards the central meridian line of the body.

» 2–4 Clear Quartz points placed around the top of the head, pointing away from the head.

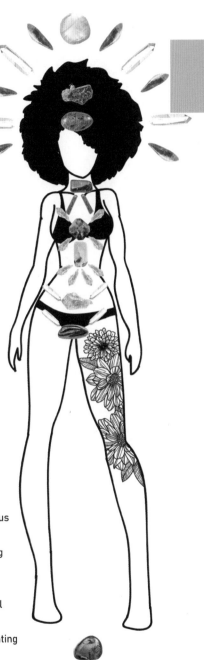

THE HEALING

Anger can be caused by many different triggers. Sometimes the triggers seem so minor and insignificant that it can be impossible to understand why such a heated response is even necessary. Occasionally, feelings of constant or frequent anger can boil over into our personal and professional lives, affecting our relationships and our ability to act rationally and clearly.

Even though anger has an infinite number of triggers, there are actually limited root causes. Almost certainly, if we trace an angry outburst back to its source, we will find that its roots lie in fear, pain and disconnection. Although this does not excuse the hurtful actions of an angry outburst, it does provide us with a positive platform from which to start the healing process.

The key energies and qualities we want to bring to a crystal healing session for anger are calmness, clarity, coolness, love, release and balance. This layout requires a lot of careful thought, because many 'fiery' crystals that are most commonly used at the Root, Sacral and Solar Plexus chakras (such as Carnelian, Bloodstone and Red Jasper) are unsuitable, given the focus on 'keeping cool'.

Anger is a low-vibrational response to a high-vibrational hurt. What this means is that one of our highest values has been violated somewhere along the line of our personal history. This violation has resulted in a seed of anger being planted in our psyche, which, with the right fertiliser, has sprouted and flourished over the course of many years. The original seed may have been planted in a tiny moment of feeling unloved, betrayed or humiliated in early childhood, or may be the result of a much more prolonged and painful trauma.

Because an anger response generates from the lower earthly chakras, it is important that we don't overload these energy centres with warm, fiery and stimulating crystals in this layout. Instead, we focus on using a large number of high-vibrational stones to draw the energies upwards towards Spirit. We also want to be sure to use gentle, calming and cooling stones from the Throat Chakra downwards.

Lepidolite encourages change through the gentle release of old, non-serving behaviour and psychological patterns. At the Crown Chakra, it brings calm and relaxation, tenderly releasing mental tension. Together with deeply meditative and sedative Moonstone at the Higher Crown Chakra and tranquil Chrysocolla at the Third Eye Chakra, Lepidolite acts like a psychological mood relaxant.

These three powerfully calming stones are supported by Amethyst points around the top of the head, which direct the qualities of peace and stillness into the mind.

The outward-pointing Clear Quartz points channel heat and anger away from the mind, replacing 'hot-headedness' with clarity and cleansing.

At the Throat Chakra, Sodalite and Kyanite work to open the lines of communication in a calm and clear manner. Their cool blue energies remind us to speak our truth with integrity and strength, but never with violence.

The Kyanite blades are placed strategically in this layout to bring coolness and relaxation to any tension held through the neck and shoulders.

Emerald (or Green Aventurine) at the Heart Chakra tempers and balances the emotions without the heat energy of a pink or red stone. It soothes someone who may be emotionally unstable and helps to keep emotional outbursts in check. A green Heart Chakra stone also offers a cool, calm and refreshed emotional perspective.

At the Solar Plexus Chakra, we use Chrysoprase, which is a wonderful healer of the emotions and cleanser of the physical and energetic bodies. Additionally, when used at the Solar Plexus Chakra specifically, it draws out negativity, judgement and other self-destructive emotions that may be impacting a person's emotional, mental and spiritual health. This is important, because anger is often a projection onto others based on how we view ourselves.

Because we are avoiding using 'hot' stones at the lower chakras, we use Citrine at the Sacral Chakra, instead of a more deeply orange or red stone. The Sacral Chakra is a core energy centre for harbouring anger, and Citrine represents everything that opposes anger. It is a beautiful stone full of light, positivity, joy, inspiration, cleansing and abundance. At the Sacral Chakra, it works to transmute beliefs of worthlessness into self-esteem, anger into joy and hurt into healing.

Hematite at the Root Chakra and Smoky Quartz at the Earth Chakra provide grounding and stability, while opening a pathway for blocked energy and old patterns to be released.

Because Hematite is so gravitational and pulls the energies downwards with such strength, we soften it with the addition of Smoky Quartz at the Earth Chakra.

Smoky Quartz is also excellent for helping us to overcome fear, anxiety and depression, which may be present in a person who suffers from angry outbursts.

◊ People who are full of anger and rage are often only externalising and projecting onto others the way they feel about themselves. Self-loathing and anger go hand in hand. One of the most powerful methods for helping someone to overcome their anger is to engulf them in unconditional love. It can be beautiful to introduce touch into this session by gently placing your hands over your partner's heart. With your hands resting softly on their body, send your love through the palms of your hands and into their deepest core.

◊ Ask your partner to visualise what their anger feels like. If you are working on yourself, then ponder this same question. Ask your partner to give the anger a colour, shape and form. Ask them to also describe its dimensions, weight and any feelings or energy it has. Finally, ask your partner to visualise the anger changing shape, shrinking or morphing into something different and less threatening. This process helps us to disengage from the anger and understand it as an entity separate from ourselves. We do not need to own it, nor does it define who we are. Once anger has been separated from the Self, it is much easier to release and let go.

◊ You could get even more creative with the above visualisation and ask your partner to visualise the anger turning into a balloon, which is tied to them by a string. Ask them to visualise cutting the string, then watching the anger float away. Don't be afraid to take these suggestions and experiment with your own ideas. Remember, a Spiritual Rebel doesn't always do things by the book!

◊ Calming oils, music and scents would be a great addition to this session. Frankincense, lavender, jasmine, violet and rose oils are all good choices for diffusing a hot temper. (See note on p. 118.)

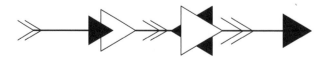

SELF-ACCEPTANCE

HEALING OUTCOMES

Increased self-esteem and confidence | Reconnecting with personal power | Release of negative projections | Self-forgiveness, love and acceptance

DIFFICULTY LEVEL

Advanced

CRYSTAL PLACEMENT

EARTH:	Grounding stone of choice (Hematite, Black Tourmaline, for example)
HIGHER CROWN:	Higher stone of choice (Clear Quartz, Selenite, for example)
CROWN:	Amethyst
THIRD EYE:	Sugilite
THROAT:	Lapis Lazuli
HEART:	Rose Quartz
SOLAR PLEXUS:	Rose Quartz
SACRAL:	Rose Quartz
ROOT:	Smoky Quartz

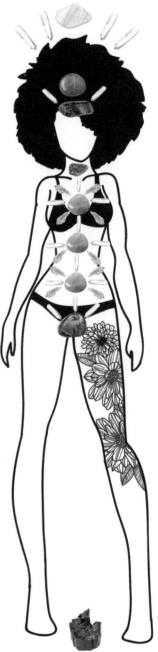

CRYSTAL POINTS

» 8–12 Citrine points placed around the Heart, Solar Plexus and Sacral chakras, pointing in towards each chakra.

» 2 Clear Quartz points placed either side of the Third Eye, Heart, Solar Plexus, Sacral and Root chakras, pointing in towards each chakra.

» 2–4 Clear Quartz points placed around the top of the head, pointing down towards the head.

» A single Clear Quartz point placed between each of the Throat, Heart, Solar Plexus, Sacral and Root chakras, all pointing down towards the Root Chakra.

THE HEALING

This layout builds on the 'Confidence and self-esteem' layout (see page 112). We learned earlier how much Rose Quartz and Citrine love working together, which is why they feature together again in this layout.

At the Crown Chakra, Amethyst connects us to our higher consciousness. This is a key aspect of working with anyone whose vibration has lowered into a state of self-loathing or self-judgement. Once any non-serving programs have been acknowledged and overcome, they can be released. What remains is the energetic space for us to develop intuition, understanding and wisdom. We are reminded that we are spiritual beings having a human experience and that we hold divinity within us.

Clear Quartz around the head supports this process. It acts as a conduit between the spiritual and physical worlds, carrying clarity, awareness and healing into our mind-space.

The cleansing properties of Quartz help us to overwrite old programming, which may have been planted so long ago that we have owned it as our own. This is especially relevant in the case of those who have been made to feel worthless so often that they have accepted this projection as truth.

At the Third Eye Chakra, Sugilite, which is a powerful stone for the emotions, promotes a deeper and more spiritually connected love experience. Rather than flushing us with romantic feelings, it permeates a much higher vibrational version of love into our being. It opens the Third Eye, so that we may view ourselves through the lens of our cosmic birth mother – as a child of the universe, worthy of unconditional love.

Lapis Lazuli has strong connections to ancient Egypt, where it was prized for its deep blue beauty and mystical properties. Resonating with the Third Eye and the Throat chakras, it stimulates intellect and understanding, honest communication, integrity and learning, so that we can learn from our mistakes, rather than continue to beat ourselves up about them. This is important for those whose feelings of self-loathing may have seeded in a perceived failure.

In order to move past our programming around 'failure', we must first understand that experiences of failure are only belief patterns, centred around expected outcomes. Once we release the expectation we place on a situation, then all experiences (both positive and negative) simply become learning opportunities for continued growth.

The Heart, Solar Plexus and Sacral chakras are all key energy centres from which we draw on our experiences to create our emotional reality. These are the chakras through which we express emotion, identity, sense of Self, Ego and vulnerabilities.

Rose Quartz on all these chakras can therefore have a profound effect by amplifying the energies of unconditional love, forgiveness and compassion. In addition, Rose Quartz can be beneficial in soothing emotional trauma and pain, while offering acceptance, kindness and support at times when we need it most.

At the Solar Plexus Chakra specifically, Rose Quartz reminds us to treat ourselves with kindness and respect, because we *are* worth loving, and we *are* worthy of receiving success and happiness.

Citrine and Clear Quartz points help to amplify this message by carrying it deep into each chakra. The result is an overall feeling of lightness, confidence, joy and abundance.

In this layout, we use Smoky Quartz at the Root Chakra, because it provides grounding without being too energetically heavy. For this reason, it is my favourite grounding stone when working with clients who are in a low-vibrational state (such as depression, self-loathing or mental anguish).

Smoky Quartz is a good friend to those who are emotionally and mentally vulnerable, because it protects against negative influences and projections from others. The risk of absorbing these negative energies is that we might allow others' judgements to shape our view of ourselves.

EXPERT TIPS

◊ Strengthen the energies of the Rose Quartz by pointing your wand tip at the Citrine points and tracing along their length towards each chakra. Doing this channels energy from the Citrine points into the Rose Quartz.

◊ If you are performing this layout on yourself, visualise gold energy warming up your heart-space from within. Feel this warm, gold light shining throughout your whole body, filling you with a deep sense of love, joy and acceptance. You can create a gold-themed guided visualisation for your partner too!

◊   Any focused Heart Chakra and Solar Plexus Chakra work can be very emotional. Always have tissues on hand and provide as much support as possible to your partner during and after the session.

◊   This is another layout where lots of physical touch can take the healing to the next level. Remember, those with low self-esteem may not receive much touch from others, or they may receive a lot of 'empty' touch (touch without love or acceptance). Place your hands lightly over your partner's Heart and Solar Plexus chakras and send your unconditional love into these energy centres.

◊   Encourage your partner to recite some positive mantras such as 'I am worthy of giving and receiving love in giant proportions'.

◊   Add Tiger's Eye to the Solar Plexus and Sacral chakras for extra self-confidence, power and courage.

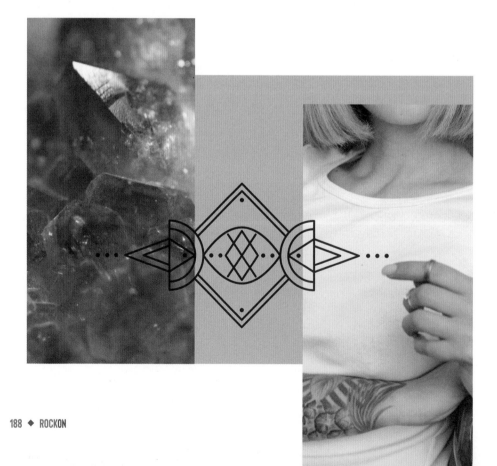

PREGNANCY AND FERTILITY

HEALING OUTCOMES

Preparing the body energetically for pregnancy | Healing
support through fertility treatments and IVF | Enhancing
the fertile window of opportunity for pregnancy

DIFFICULTY LEVEL

Advanced

CRYSTAL PLACEMENT

EARTH:	Grounding stone of choice (Hematite, Smoky Quartz, for example)
HIGHER CROWN:	Higher stone of choice (Selenite, Clear Quartz, for example)
HEART:	Rose Quartz
SOLAR PLEXUS:	Rose Quartz
SACRAL:	Moonstone
WOMB:	Moonstone placed directly over the womb (uterus)
OVARIES:	Rose Quartz placed over each ovary
ROOT:	Shiva Lingam

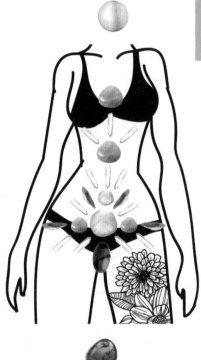

CRYSTAL POINTS

» 4–8 Amethyst points placed around the womb and ovaries, pointing inwards towards the main stones.

» 6–8 Clear Quartz points placed around the womb and ovaries, pointing inwards towards the main stones.

» 3 Clear Quartz points placed just above each of the Solar Plexus and Sacral chakras, pointing in towards the chakra and angled downwards.

THE HEALING

There are many factors that affect fertility so, for this layout to be most successful, it is important to determine whether there are any underlying health issues that may be affecting your partner's ability to get pregnant. These may include eating disorders, irregular menstrual cycles, substance abuse, polycystic ovarian syndrome (PCOS) or endometriosis. For this reason, it is important to remain optimistically realistic about what we can achieve using crystal healing alone.

This layout is ideally performed on a woman with no underlying biological risk factors and who is at the start of her pregnancy journey. The goal is to provide fertility support and promote a speedier conception and healthier pregnancy.

Rose Quartz and Moonstone are two of the most powerful and effective fertility stones in the mineral kingdom, which is why we place them directly over the reproductive organs in this layout.

IMPORTANT

Before starting this healing, we must be clear that this layout should be used *only* as a supportive tool for a woman who is trying to get pregnant and who has *not* been traumatised by the pregnancy process.

Please keep in mind that infertility, miscarriage and pregnancy loss are all incredibly energetically traumatic experiences that are best processed with an experienced healing practitioner.

I never recommend performing a crystal healing on a woman who is pregnant (unless you are an advanced crystal healer), because developing babies are highly sensitive to energetic frequencies.

Because Rose Quartz embodies the maternal qualities of unconditional love, patience, acceptance, forgiveness and support, it is my personal favourite when working with mothers-to-be.

Moonstone is a close second, because it resonates with the moon and lunar energies, which naturally connect with the female monthly fertility cycle. It is also the mineral embodiment of the Divine Feminine.

By working with Rose Quartz on the Heart and Solar Plexus chakras, we are creating emotional support for a woman who may have been trying to get pregnant for a while, or, only if you are an advanced healer, for a woman who has suffered a pregnancy-related trauma, such as miscarriage.

Rose Quartz also brings maternal healing in the form of unconditional love, which resonates with a woman's heart's desire to become a mother. Clear Quartz points at the Solar Plexus Chakra amplify and strengthen this energy.

Moonstone at the Sacral Chakra resonates with the woman's physical body and natural moon-cycle to maximise her fertile energy. Some crystal healers recommend using Carnelian as a fertility stone here. However, because of its powerful cleansing and detoxification properties, I never use Carnelian (or any detoxification stone) on the belly of a woman who is trying to become pregnant. If there is a possibility that she may already be pregnant (without knowing), strong detoxification stones may trigger miscarriage in some rare instances.

Shiva Lingam comes from India and represents the penis of the god Shiva. It is said to contain the power of the Divine Masculine and is a popular stone for male fertility and virility. I described this stone in the layout for male sexual health (see page 147); however, we can also use it when working on women in certain healing situations. This includes crystal layouts for channelling Divine Masculine energy.

The use of this stone over the Root Chakra (or at the entrance to the vagina if you are working on a close friend or lover) is to support the woman's receptiveness to sperm. The Shiva Lingam honours the masculine role in conception, via the sperm, and brings energetic strength and stamina to their journey. This is especially important for low sperm count or sperm that is compromised in quality. For best results, this layout should be performed within 24 hours of intercourse.

Amethyst and Clear Quartz points around the reproductive organs help to amplify the energy of the fertility stones for maximum result.

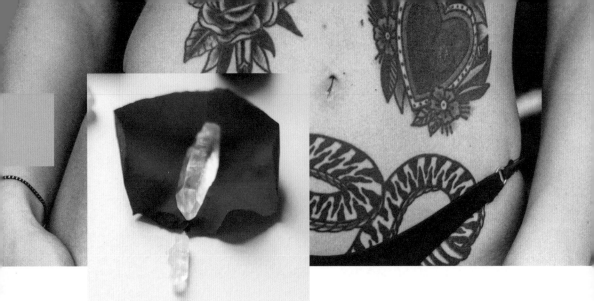

EXPERT TIPS

◊ Ideally, this layout is best performed in the fertile window of a partner's menstrual cycle, which is usually between days 9 and 14. Please keep in mind that the window will vary from woman to woman, so it should be mapped accurately for each individual.

◊ Place your hands gently over your partner's womb and take her on a guided visualisation that focuses on the concepts of life and birth. For example, you may like to ask her to visualise planting a seed of a fruit tree in a beautiful garden, then watching it grow and ripen.

◊ As mentioned earlier, it is not advisable to place grounding or cleansing stones on any chakras (other than the Earth Chakra) on a woman who is trying to get pregnant. This includes (but is not limited to) Hematite, Bloodstone, Carnelian, Red Jasper, Black Obsidian and Black Tourmaline.

◊ If you or your partner are receiving IVF treatment or artificial insemination, then this layout should be performed within 24 hours of the implantation/insemination procedure for best results.

FEAR

HEALING OUTCOMES

Overcoming fear and phobias | Identification and release of fear-based programming | Identification and release of fear-based success blockers | Support for times of fear-based instability (such as fear of being alone after a break-up or fear of financial insecurity during periods of unemployment) | Transformation of fear into fuel for growth

DIFFICULTY LEVEL

Advanced

CRYSTAL PLACEMENT

EARTH:	Black Tourmaline and a Selenite stick placed vertically below it
HIGHER CROWN:	Selenite stick placed vertically
THIRD EYE:	Amethyst
HIGHER HEART:	Amazonite
HEART:	Rose Quartz
SOLAR PLEXUS:	Citrine
SACRAL:	Smoky Quartz
ROOT:	Black Obsidian

CRYSTAL POINTS

» 2–4 Amethyst points placed around the Higher Crown, pointing inwards towards the head.

» 2–4 Citrine points placed around the Solar Plexus Chakra, pointing in towards the chakra.

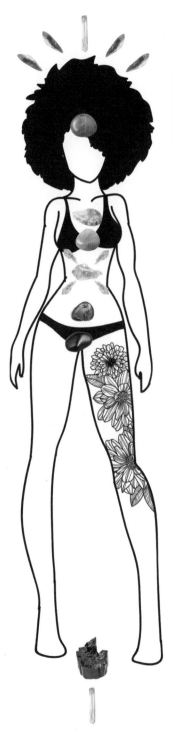

THE HEALING

This layout is a powerful healing experience for those weighed down by fear-based energy. Because fear carries a heavy vibration, it is important that we choose grounding stones that are not too heavy in themselves and that support the fear-release process.

It is also a good idea to balance the grounding stones with the much higher vibrational Selenite, which is why we place Selenite and Black Tourmaline together at the Earth Chakra.

Black Tourmaline is well known as a stone of protection. It is also compelling in bringing fear-based programming to the surface of our consciousness, so that we can acknowledge and release it.

Selenite supports and softens the fear-release process (which can be terrifying and confronting) by bringing a much higher dimensional understanding to anything unpleasant that is cast into our awareness. From this perspective, we can regard and process it with wisdom and support from our highest levels of consciousness.

Black Obsidian and Smoky Quartz work together on the lower chakras to help ground and stabilise fearful energies.

Black Obsidian supports the Root Chakra, which provides a safe elimination point for fear to be released. It also acts as an energetic and psychic filter, protecting us from dark and depressive thoughts, which often grow like weeds in a garden of fear.

At the Solar Plexus Chakra, Citrine fills us with light-energy. It helps us to overcome fear and self-doubt by shining with vitality and confidence. A powerful ally when working with fear, it reminds us of our ability to focus on the 'bright side', rather than letting fear rule our decision-making.

The Citrine points that face upwards keep the flow of energy travelling towards the higher chakras, opposing the low-vibrational energy of fear in the lower chakras.

At the Heart Chakra, Rose Quartz provides comfort, love, support and emotional strength as we explore thoughts and feelings that may frighten us.

Amazonite at the Higher Heart Chakra clears a path for our feelings to connect with the Throat Chakra. This encourages us to be brave enough to speak our truth and follow our heart's desires.

Amazonite also helps us to overcome any fear of conflict and brings emotional clarity and protection at times when these qualities elude us.

At the Third Eye Chakra (and the points around the Higher Crown), Amethyst helps us overcome any fear-based blocks that might be rooted in our mental or spiritual programming. It opens the doorway to our Highest Self, so that we can see situations with clear vision and intuition, freeing ourselves from the cloudy darkness of fear.

Once we have regained perspective and clarity, we are much more able to approach intimidating situations with wisdom and understanding (instead of fear and defensiveness). We can also confidently focus on our path ahead without fear-based obstructions blocking the way.

The addition of Selenite (supported by Amethyst) at the Higher Crown assists in lifting us out of the dark and heavy energy that comes with a fear-based mentality.

It is important to work with the natural alignment of Selenite by placing it vertically above the head. This ensures that the high-vibrational energies are flowing upwards through the Higher Crown Chakra.

Once we have reached our highest possible level of awareness and understanding, we can realise our true purpose and move forward with lightness and freedom, no longer bound by the chains of fear.

EXPERT TIPS

◊ Always focus on lightness when working on fear. Use white sheets, focus on white healing light in visualisations and give your partner some Amethyst to keep close by afterwards. This will provide energetic and psychic protection if they feel vulnerable.

◊ Because this can be an emotional and scary journey, you may like to invite your partner to select a couple of crystals to hold for support during the healing session.

◊ A powerful visualisation would complement this layout beautifully. For example, if your partner is afraid of heights, you may take them through a guided visualisation that involves slowly climbing up some steps at the side of a mountain. The view from the top should be exhilarating and empowering, and, with your reassurance, they should feel perfectly safe and secure every step of the way.

LETTING GO

HEALING OUTCOMES

Releasing a painful past | Support for moving on from a traumatic life event | Release of non-serving emotions such as bitterness, guilt, resentment, blame, betrayal, sadness and prolonged grief | Getting unstuck from a rut | Support through unexpected transition and change

DIFFICULTY LEVEL

Advanced

CRYSTAL PLACEMENT

EARTH:	Orthoceras
HIGHER CROWN:	Clear Quartz (good stone clarity is important for this layout)
CROWN:	Lepidolite
THIRD EYE:	Sodalite
HIGHER HEART:	Chrysocolla
HEART:	Labradorite (centre) with a Rose Quartz on either side
SOLAR PLEXUS:	Citrine (upper) and Chiastolite (lower)
SACRAL:	Bloodstone
ROOT:	Smoky Quartz

CRYSTAL POINTS

> » 2–4 Amethyst points placed around the top of the head, pointing down towards the head.
> » 2–4 Clear Quartz points placed around the top of the head, pointing away from the head.
> » 3 Clear Quartz points placed at the Heart, Sacral and Root chakras, pointing in towards each chakra and angled downwards.
> » 4 Citrine points placed around the Solar Plexus Chakra, pointing in towards the chakra.

THE HEALING

This is a powerful healing layout for those needing to let go and release old pain and trauma. It is particularly beneficial for clearing the pathway for moving forward with renewed direction, freedom and positivity.

This layout can be used for a wide range of situations, and is thorough in supporting and releasing all the main energy centres where trauma and blocked energy may build up.

There are three main outcomes that we are working towards in this layout: release from the past; healing for the present; and clarity, confidence and freedom for the future.

At the Earth Chakra, we have Orthoceras. As explained in the 'Resolving the past' layout (see page 154), Orthoceras is excellent for connecting us with our past and helping us to accept situations beyond our control. In this layout specifically, it assists us in accepting the outcome of past events that we have found ourselves unable to move on from. This might include our personal history, our physicality and our mortality.

Orthoceras raises the ideas of death, rebirth, preservation and life cycles, anchoring the energy of these concepts into our foundational chakra. From here, it can be processed and integrated for our continued personal evolution. It also brings into reality the idea that some things naturally must end or die, so that we can evolve.

Smoky Quartz at the Root Chakra and Bloodstone at the Sacral Chakra help with the cleansing and release process. Both crystals work to draw blocked energy downwards for release while simultaneously cleansing the lower chakras. Smoky Quartz works more on the energetic level, while Bloodstone works more on the physical level.

Smoky Quartz is also an amazing stone for helping us overcome depression, addiction and other heavy emotional weights that we may find ourselves unable to detach from.

We use quite a complex combination of stones at the Solar Plexus and Heart chakras. Most of the time, when we find ourselves unable or unwilling to let go or move on from something, it is because we have a significant emotional investment in it. This is frequently understandable, especially if we are grieving the death of a loved one or the loss of a meaningful relationship.

Initially, it may be difficult to understand our emotional investment in beliefs or behaviours that don't benefit our quality of life. One example of this might be harbouring feelings of resentment towards a person who wronged us a long time ago. Nevertheless, there is almost always an underlying emotional attachment to any behaviour or pattern, and this attachment keeps us in a state of inertia, unable to let go and move forward with life.

Keeping all this in mind, we should be discerning in our use of crystals in this layout. At the Solar Plexus Chakra, we use Chiastolite as a tool for facilitating change, new direction and transition, as well as providing emotional stability.

Citrine shines a light into the darkness that may have descended upon our world, helping to release us from fear and uncertainty.

The Solar Plexus Chakra acts like a mirror (or gateway) to how we view ourselves. Chiastolite and Citrine used here also help reflect the *need* for decisiveness and change, so that we can create a brighter future for ourselves.

It's important to make sure your partner feels emotionally ready and supported through the letting go process. They are about to take a potentially terrifying step out of their comfort zone, which is where Rose Quartz, Chrysocolla and Labradorite come into play.

Rose Quartz gently opens the Heart Chakra and provides comfort and support, while Chrysocolla soothes and sedates a fearful mind.

Labradorite helps us to draw wisdom from our experiences and understand ourselves on a much deeper level. Understanding is a vital step towards acceptance. And acceptance is a vital step towards letting go.

At the higher chakras, Sodalite brings much-needed clarity and calm, while Lepidolite bathes us in the warmth of universal love and connectedness.

To commit to the letting go process, we need to see the path ahead clearly. Clear Quartz at the Higher Crown helps this process, which is why we want to use as clear a Quartz crystal as possible. It also works to open the doorway to our higher consciousness, so that we can rise above and be unburdened from our earthly attachments.

EXPERT TIPS

◊   Rituals are one of the most powerful methods for facilitating the letting go experience. A simple ritual could involve asking your partner to write a few words on a piece of paper to represent what they are holding on to. With your support and guidance, invite your partner to burn the paper over a candle flame. As the paper burns and the smoke lifts, ask them to feel the weight of their attachment being carried away with the rising smoke.

ADDICTION

HEALING OUTCOMES

Release from addictive mindsets and urges | Awareness of addictive 'crutches' in our life | Encouragement to find freedom from emotional, behavioural and physical dependencies

DIFFICULTY LEVEL

Advanced

CRYSTAL PLACEMENT

EARTH: Hematite
HIGHER CROWN: Clear Quartz
CROWN: Amethyst
THIRD EYE: Amethyst
HIGHER HEART: Watermelon Tourmaline
HEART: Rose Quartz
SOLAR PLEXUS: Citrine
SACRAL: Carnelian
ROOT: Bloodstone (upper) and Hematite (lower)

CRYSTAL POINTS

- » 2–4 Amethyst points placed around the top of the head, pointing down towards the head.
- » 2–4 Clear Quartz points placed around the top of the head, pointing away from the head.
- » 4 Citrine points placed around the Heart Chakra, pointing in towards the heart.
- » A single Clear Quartz point placed below the Solar Plexus Chakra, pointing down towards the Sacral Chakra.
- » 2 Amethyst points angled downwards, pointing towards the Sacral Chakra.
- » 2 Clear Quartz points angled downwards, pointing towards the Root Chakra.

THE HEALING

This layout combines three main healing elements: support and strength to overcome addiction; positive self-image; and detoxification. The key stones in this grid that assist in overcoming addiction are Amethyst, Citrine, Clear Quartz and Watermelon Tourmaline.

In ancient Greece, Amethyst was widely believed to protect its owner against the effects of alcohol. In fact, the word 'amethyst' comes from the ancient Greek 'amethustos', which literally means 'not drunk'. This makes it one of the most effective stones for detoxifying the energetic body from substance and alcohol addiction.

The high-vibrational energy of Amethyst works to lift awareness out of the low-vibrational, physical craving of addiction and into a higher plane. Amethyst cleanses and purifies the blood, calms the mind and brings awareness and wisdom to our decision-making.

Clear Quartz is also an incredibly cleansing crystal. It purifies on all levels and connects us to the highest version of ourselves, so that we might experience clarity and healing.

At the Higher Heart Chakra, Watermelon Tourmaline helps us to break old patterns of thinking and behaviour. It is an excellent stone for healing if the goal is to overcome the old and embrace the new. It supports us emotionally and helps us to maintain emotional balance as we grapple with our non-serving needs.

Watermelon Tourmaline can be difficult and expensive to source, so Ruby in Zoisite would be a suitable substitute in this layout.

Citrine is arguably as powerful as Amethyst for overcoming addiction, because it instils in us self-confidence, radiance, positivity and the strength to overcome our urges and desires.

A little-known fact about Citrine is that it is birthed from Amethyst. When an Amethyst crystal is continually subjected to heat and pressure, it begins to transform and shift from purple to yellow. An Amethyst that is part-way through this transition is called Ametrine, which holds the qualities of both Amethyst and Citrine in its energetic core.

Citrine married with Rose Quartz and Watermelon Tourmaline at the heart bathes us in the energies of love and forgiveness when we are at our most vulnerable.

This layout encourages us to be kind to ourselves and also raises our sense of self-worth and self-regard. In this way, we are less likely to succumb to our addictions, which often originate from a place of self-loathing, disconnection, worthlessness and emptiness.

Carnelian at the Sacral Chakra infuses the physical body with the strength and stamina to 'go the distance', helping us to abstain from our vices.

Additionally, Carnelian is an effective detoxification stone, used to cleanse toxins from the physical and energetic body. The dislodged toxic energy is channelled down towards the Root Chakra, via the downward pointing Quartz points, for release.

Bloodstone and Hematite at the Root Chakra work to magnetically draw all the toxins earthwards to be eliminated. As their names suggest, they are both stones that resonate with the blood, helping to cleanse and purify on a cellular energetic level.

Hematite brings the extra quality of mental clarity and focus, which helps us to remain psychologically strong as we separate ourselves from the mental trap of addiction.

EXPERT TIPS

◊ This layout is best performed on a regular basis. Overcoming addiction can be a long process and your partner will need lots of support along the way.

◊ Extra touch by way of Reiki and gentle hand placement over the Heart and Solar Plexus chakras can be exceptionally powerful in this layout. Send your highest love and light intentions into your partner through the palms of your hands.

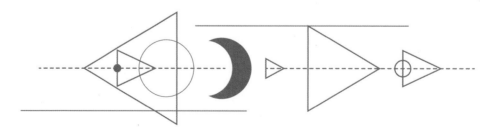

LOVE

HEALING OUTCOMES

Release from emotional trauma and heartache | Opening of the
Heart Chakra | Acceptance, trust, love and forgiveness | Emotional
support and connection | Attracting a soulmate or partner |
Reconnecting to the emotional self | Acceptance of vulnerability

DIFFICULTY LEVEL

Advanced

CRYSTAL PLACEMENT

EARTH:	Grounding stone of choice (Obsidian, Hematite, for example)
HIGHER CROWN:	Clear Quartz
CROWN:	Amethyst
THIRD EYE:	Lepidolite (purple or pink)
THROAT:	Turquoise
HIGHER HEART:	Rhodochrosite
HEART:	Rose Quartz
SOLAR PLEXUS:	Rose Quartz
SACRAL:	Garnet
ROOT:	Smoky Quartz

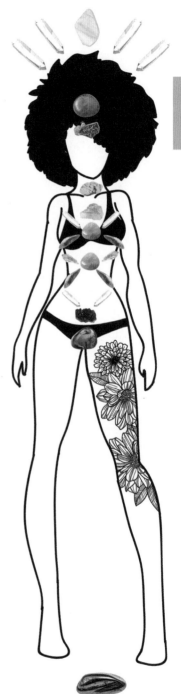

CRYSTAL POINTS

» 4–6 Clear Quartz points placed around the top of the head,
   pointing down towards the head.
» 2 Clear Quartz points placed just above and either side of the
   Heart Chakra, pointing down towards the heart.
» 2 Amethyst points placed just below and either side of the
   Heart Chakra, pointing up towards the heart.
» 2 Citrine points placed just above the Solar Plexus Chakra,
   pointing down towards the chakra.

- » 2 Amethyst points placed just below the Solar Plexus Chakra, pointing up towards the chakra.
- » 2 Clear Quartz points placed just above the Sacral Chakra, angled downwards, pointing towards the chakra.

THE HEALING

This layout radiates with love, support, self-confidence and emotional healing, which are all key qualities when it comes to inviting love into our life. So often, we need to heal and learn to love ourselves, before we can truly experience love from another.

The layout begins with Clear Quartz points around the head, drawing the energies inwards (for attraction). We want to harness all that cosmic, higher consciousness energy that Clear Quartz connects us to, so that we can cleanse our mind of negative and self-sabotaging thoughts. This will enable us to experience psychological and emotional healing, as well as making our truest intentions known to the universe.

Clear Quartz is a wonderful manifestation stone, because it can be individually programmed with our own specific intentions for the healing. This means we can imprint the crystals with our highest intention for love, before we even begin working with them.

Amethyst at the Crown Chakra (as well as in a supportive role at the Heart and Solar Plexus chakras) and Lepidolite at the Third Eye Chakra keep our intentions pure and high-vibrational. This is not a layout to attract lustful liaisons! Rather, we aim to magnetise a deep, spiritually fulfilling love, and feel it shine throughout our entire being.

Amethyst also assists us in identifying obstacles that might be sabotaging our highest expression of love.

At the Throat Chakra, Turquoise works to bring clear communication and protection from emotional pain (excellent for those who are heart-shy), while keeping our truth and integrity intact. It is also known as the friendship stone, because its vibration attracts like-minded souls to us for connection and friendship. Friendship is, of course, the perfect garden for love to blossom!

In position at the Higher Heart, Rhodochrosite is a master healer. It gently encourages us to release emotional trauma and heal old wounds, so that we can trust again.

Rose Quartz at the Heart and Solar Plexus chakras reminds us that we are spiritual beings capable of giving and receiving infinite quantities of love. It energetically supports and balances the emotions, gently opening the Heart Chakra to teach us

about love, forgiveness, compassion, kindness and acceptance. At the Solar Plexus Chakra, this translates into a more accepting and loving view of ourselves.

At the Sacral Chakra, Garnet awakens the energies of passion, vitality and success. It fills us with a feeling of readiness to welcome a romantic partner, which can be subliminally sensed by those around us.

Smoky Quartz at the Root Chakra helps ground and protect, warding off those who might seek to take advantage of our emotional vulnerability.

EXPERT TIPS

◊ Place your hands over your partner's Heart Chakra and spend some time channelling focused love-energy into their heart-space. It can be powerful medicine to simply sit in this space and send another person unconditional love, because love is too often based on expectations and conditions.

◊ Invite your partner to start each day by looking in the mirror and reciting some positive mantras, such as 'I am worthy of giving and receiving an abundance of love'.

EMOTIONAL TRAUMA

HEALING OUTCOMES

Release from emotional trauma | Healing support after losing
a loved one | Support to move on emotionally after heartbreak |
Release from negative emotional patterns and behaviour |
Support through grief, emotional turmoil and emotional abuse

DIFFICULTY LEVEL

Advanced

CRYSTAL PLACEMENT

EARTH:	Grounding stone of choice (Obsidian, Hematite, for example)
HIGHER CROWN:	Selenite
CROWN:	Amethyst
THIRD EYE:	Lapis Lazuli
HIGHER HEART:	Aquamarine
HEART:	Rose Quartz (upper) and Chrysocolla (lower)
SOLAR PLEXUS:	Malachite
ROOT:	Smoky Quartz

CRYSTAL POINTS

» 4–6 Clear Quartz points placed around the top of the head, pointing down towards the head.

» A single Clear Quartz point placed at the Throat Chakra, pointing down towards the heart.

» 2–4 Clear Quartz points placed at each of the chakras in the layout, pointing in towards the chakra.

» 2–4 Amethyst points placed around the Heart Chakra, pointing in towards the heart.

» 2–4 Citrine points placed around the Solar Plexus Chakra, pointing in towards the chakra.

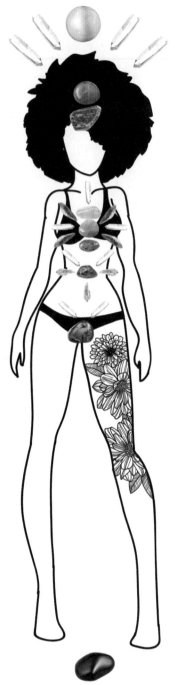

THE HEALING

Because it can be painful and emotional to process traumatic experiences, it is extremely important that your partner is completely supported during and after this healing.

Our choice of stones in this layout needs to be both effective and subtle to minimise any sudden and unexpected emotional pain. We want to release and heal the emotions softly, not create more trauma by treading too heavily through our partner's heart-space.

Although the focus of this layout is on healing the Heart and Solar Plexus chakras, we also need to honour and support the psychological body, using Amethyst, Lapis Lazuli, Selenite and Clear Quartz.

These high-vibrational healing stones bring understanding and acceptance to an emotionally painful situation. They also work well together to cast illumination on painful events that have transpired, so we can view them in a more cosmic and expanded light.

When we disengage emotionally from our burdens, we become more of an observer to what is essentially a subjective emotional experience. This process of separation, witnessing and expansion helps us to understand the 'bigger picture'.

At the Crown Chakra, Amethyst energetically calms and sedates, shifting our perspective to one more in alignment with our spiritual belief system.

At the Third Eye Chakra, Lapis Lazuli shines truth into our awareness, while also helping us to regard our emotional pain with insight.

Aquamarine at the Higher Heart Chakra works to bring harmony to emotional disputes and imbalance. It is a stone named after the colour of the sea. Just like the gentle ebb and flow of the ocean tides, Aquamarine energetically washes away pain and heartache, replacing it with compassion. It also helps us to release that which no longer serves.

Rose Quartz and Chrysocolla are also delicate heart-healers and play an important role at the Heart Chakra in balancing the strength of Malachite at the Solar Plexus Chakra.

Malachite is one of the most powerful protection stones in the mineral kingdom. It can be used to create a protective shield around us when we feel vulnerable, but it works like an energetic sponge. It penetrates quickly and deeply into the emotional layers to effectively soak up and draw out energetic trauma and pain. This trauma is then cast into our awareness, whether we are ready to face the feelings or not! Malachite can be quite unpleasant for those who are not prepared for such intensity, so it is vital to work gently. When working on emotional trauma, it is important to offset the intensity of Malachite with the addition of very gentle stones, like Rose Quartz and Chrysocolla.

Unlike Malachite, which can be sudden and strong, Rose Quartz and Chrysocolla are soft and nurturing. Their energy seeps gently through our emotional layers to bring soft release, inner peace, acceptance and love.

Amethyst points in a supportive role at the Heart Chakra create a space of safety in which we can deeply explore our emotional and painful feelings. It is important for an emotionally vulnerable partner to know that their experience is held sacred with unconditional support, confidentiality and understanding.

Clear Quartz points energise and amplify the heart-healing, working to cleanse and balance on all levels.

Citrine points at the Solar Plexus Chakra bring light, joy and confidence to those who may be emotionally broken. It reminds us that we can experience joy and inspiration again, and that, even in the darkest emotional corners, light may penetrate. Citrine's very nature can assist us in transmuting painful energies into something positive.

At the Root Chakra, Smoky Quartz anchors the healing into the physical body and provides energetic protection. It cleanses, helping to remove pain, and stabilises the energies that have become unsettled because of emotional trauma.

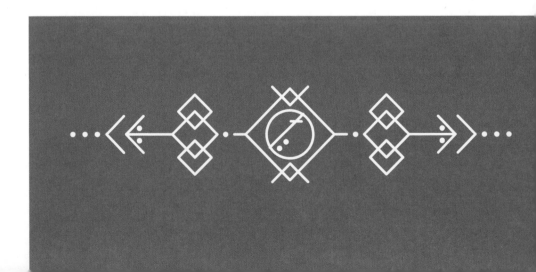

EXPERT TIPS

◊ Extra touch by way of Reiki and gentle hand placement over the Heart and Solar Plexus chakras can be exceptionally powerful in this layout. Send your highest love and light intentions into your partner through the palms of your hands.

◊ Add a communication stone to the Throat (such as Blue Lace Agate or Turquoise) if your partner struggles to talk about their feelings or communicate in their relationships.

◊ Always thoroughly cleanse Malachite after each use as it stores all the energies it absorbs, including the negative ones.

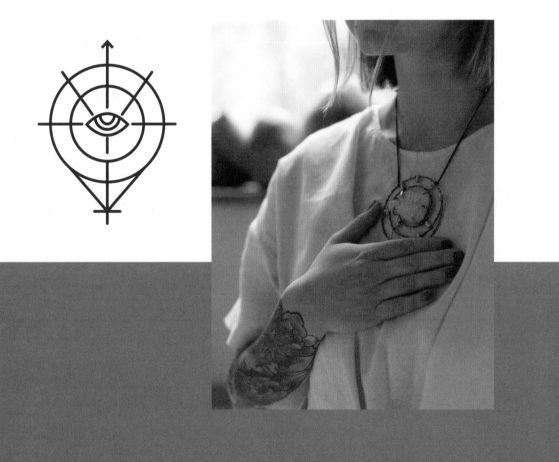

SEXUAL TRAUMA

HEALING OUTCOMES

Release from emotional and energetic trauma associated with sexual abuse | Healing support after sexual trauma | Release from feelings of shame towards the body or sex | Support for healthier sexual experiences

DIFFICULTY LEVEL

Advanced

CRYSTAL PLACEMENT

EARTH:	Grounding stone of choice (Obsidian, Hematite, for example)
HIGHER CROWN:	Selenite
CROWN:	Amethyst
THIRD EYE:	Lapis Lazuli
THROAT:	Blue Lace Agate
HIGHER HEART:	Rose Quartz
HEART:	Rhodonite (upper) and Watermelon Tourmaline (lower)
SOLAR PLEXUS:	Turquoise
SACRAL:	Carnelian (upper) and Red Garnet (lower)
ROOT:	Smoky Quartz (upper) and Black Tourmaline (lower)

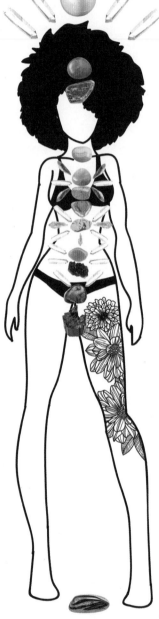

CRYSTAL POINTS

» 4–6 Clear Quartz points placed around the top of the head, pointing down towards the head.

» 2–4 Clear Quartz points placed at each of the chakras in the layout, pointing in towards the chakra.

» 2–4 Amethyst points placed around the Heart Chakra, pointing in towards the heart.

» 2–4 Citrine points placed around the Solar Plexus Chakra, pointing in towards the chakra.

THE HEALING

This layout works in a similar way to the 'Emotional trauma' layout (see page 206); however, the stones we use are quite different. One notable difference is the use of Rhodonite as the main Heart Chakra stone.

Rhodonite is one of the most effective stones for supporting acute emotional distress and trauma. It works energetically on the emotional body to help release feelings of anger, hatred and resentment, which fester beneath the surface and eat away at the soul. Acknowledgement and release of these toxic feelings is a key step towards healing for those who have experienced sexual trauma or violation.

Energetically, Rhodonite sinks deep into the emotional layers to encourage forgiveness and help us realise our full emotional potential, despite our deep scars.

Rose Quartz enhances this process by supporting, nurturing and forgiving. Being energetically connected to Rose Quartz feels like being wrapped up in an emotional cocoon of unconditional love. In this layout, it holds us safely, so that we can explore our most painful experiences with energetic support.

Watermelon Tourmaline is also an emotional healer. It helps to free us from the shackles of emotional pain and programming that has been implanted in us and, in doing so, it provides emotional freedom and release from painful experiences.

Blue Lace Agate at the Throat Chakra promotes expression and communication. It can be extremely difficult for victims of sexual trauma to find the courage and the words to speak of their experience. The truth can be stifled by complex feelings of shame, pain, guilt and fear. For this reason, we need to find a way to softly open the Throat Chakra, so that the truth can be spoken whenever your partner feels ready to do so.

Blue Lace Agate is gentle but strong. It won't 'force' anything to the surface that isn't ready to be revealed. Rather, it will gently encourage and relax the Throat Chakra, promoting a feeling of trust and safety, so that the truth can flow freely.

Sexual trauma is a terrible experience with a lot of forcefulness attached to it, so, whatever we do, we want to tread gently and supportively in this layout. Use stones that work softly, and do not press for sudden feelings or realisations.

While the emotional healing is occurring at the Heart Chakra, Turquoise at the Solar Plexus Chakra helps protect and give voice to our feelings. Although it is most commonly used at the Throat and Higher Heart chakras, in this layout we place it at the Solar Plexus Chakra to encourage release of a distorted sense of Self, which can manifest after sexual trauma.

Turquoise is known for bringing truth and clarity to the vision we hold of ourselves and reminds us to not own what is not ours. It helps to protect and keep intact all that is essentially 'us', and discards that which is not.

The Solar Plexus Chakra is also supported by Citrine, whose light chases away the shadows of our past to illuminate the brilliance that we contain within.

Citrine also works on the energetic level to help us find the strength to overcome depression, despair and addiction. It can provide the energetic support we need to lift ourselves out of pain and darkness, so that we may shine once again.

Through the lower chakras, we have an intense cleansing and clearing layout. Carnelian energetically supports healing of the sexual organs and raises kundalini energy, connecting us to our own Divine sensuality and sexuality. It works to cleanse the lower body and brings vitality, energy and sexual reawakening in an area that may have become energetically lifeless and closed.

Garnet and Carnelian draw out energetic blockage and trauma in the physical body, so that we can be free from their burdens.

Garnet is renowned as a stone for love, passion and sensuality. It helps us reconnect with ourselves sexually and intimately, so that we may share this sacred part of ourselves in a healthy and meaningful way with others. It connects the physical body and earthly desires with the spiritual realm, bringing higher consciousness to our romantic relationships for a more spiritually fulfilling experience.

At the Root Chakra, we use Smoky Quartz and Black Tourmaline for their grounding and protective qualities. Those who are working through emotional and sexual trauma are exceptionally vulnerable and need to be energetically protected while they explore their feelings. Both Smoky Quartz and Black Tourmaline assist in cleansing and stabilising unsettled energy while protecting from emotional and spiritual injury.

We use Clear Quartz throughout this entire grid to amplify, enhance, cleanse and heal on all levels. It also brings higher awareness and clarity to confusing and overwhelming thoughts and feelings, which ultimately benefits our path forward.

EXPERT TIPS

◊ Take your partner through a beautiful heart-focused healing visualisation filled with green, pink and gold colours.

◊ Extra touch by way of Reiki and gentle hand placement over the Heart, Solar Plexus and Sacral chakras can be exceptionally powerful in this layout. Send your highest love and light intentions into your partner through the palms of your hands. Always be sure to ask for permission before initiating any contact with a partner who has been sexually abused or traumatised.

◊ Ask your partner to place their own hands (palms down) over their Heart and/or Sacral chakras. Place your own hands softly over the top of theirs. Encourage them to send love, healing and forgiveness to themselves. You may also like to recite some positive mantras together, such as 'I am worthy of receiving and expressing the highest form of love'.

ATTENTION DEFICIT HYPERACTIVITY DISORDER (ADHD)

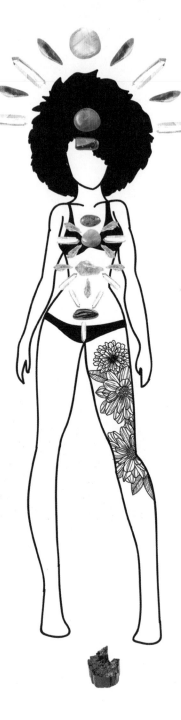

HEALING OUTCOMES

Promotion of calm, concentration and focus | Relief from an overactive or overly analytical mind | Relief from worry and obsessive thoughts | Promotion of physical relaxation and stillness | Promotion of self-confidence

DIFFICULTY LEVEL

Advanced

CRYSTAL PLACEMENT

EARTH:	Strong grounding stone (such as Black Tourmaline, Hematite or Orthoceras)
HIGHER CROWN:	Moonstone
CROWN:	Amethyst
THIRD EYE:	Sodalite
HIGHER HEART:	Chrysocolla
HEART:	Rose Quartz
SOLAR PLEXUS:	Citrine
SACRAL:	Hematite

CRYSTAL POINTS

» 2–4 Clear Quartz points placed around the top of the head, pointing away from the head.
» 2–4 Amethyst points placed around the top of the head, pointing down towards the head.
» 2–4 Clear Quartz points placed around the Heart Chakra, pointing in towards the heart.

» 4–6 Citrine points placed around the Heart and Solar Plexus chakras, pointing in towards the chakras.

» 2 Clear Quartz points placed just above the Sacral Chakra, pointing down towards the sacral stone.

» A single Clear Quartz point placed below the Sacral Chakra, pointing down towards the Root Chakra.

THE HEALING

This layout is suitable for people of all ages (including children over the age of six). If you are working with a small child, then only leave the crystals on for a maximum of 15 minutes and, if the child is quite wriggly, remove most of the crystal points.

Much of what distinguishes a person with ADHD is an overactive mind, physical hyperactivity and a lack of impulse control. This can result in a lot of negative feedback from the outside world, which can, in turn, lead to negative self-image and even worse behaviour. In this layout, the key healing objectives are to instil calmness, focus and positive self-image.

This is one of the more complex head layouts. In this layout, we need to be extra mindful of the additional energies we are introducing into what might be a chaotic mind-space.

We have Moonstone at the Higher Crown Chakra, which resonates with the moon and celestial energies. This is excellent for encouraging mental calm and deep sleep, and providing a beacon of light in times of darkness.

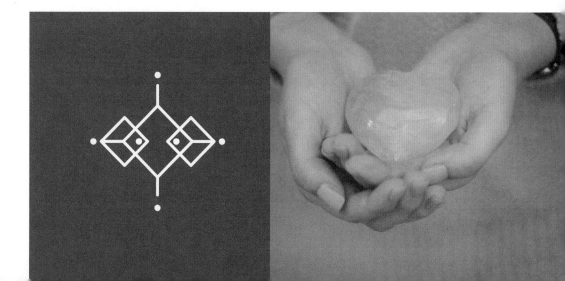

The soft Moonstone energy is complemented by inward-facing Amethyst points, which are in place to channel stillness, tranquillity and contemplation into the head area, and Amethyst at the Crown Chakra. The outward-facing Clear Quartz points draw out mental clutter, stress and busy thoughts.

Sodalite at the Third Eye Chakra brings an additional calming dimension to the head layout, penetrating deep into the energetic and mental layers to bring stillness, clarity and focus. It helps those who are prone to overthinking to switch off and find peace from their own demanding thoughts.

What we hope to achieve through this head layout is clarity and spaciousness in a cluttered mind. Clear Quartz and Sodalite can also assist those who are hypersensitive to electromagnetic stress (such as from TVs and computers). This seems to be a common complaint for those with ADHD, whose neural frequencies can be extreme, making them potentially more susceptible to electromagnetic fields (EMFs).

At the Higher Heart Chakra, Chrysocolla works to calm and cleanse. Its soothing and constant vibration stabilises volatile and turbulent emotions, replacing them with tranquillity. It cools 'hot' emotional outbursts and brings balance to those who are prone to moodiness.

Rose Quartz at the Heart Chakra is greatly important, because it is one of the most accepting and loving of all stones. This energy of unconditional love is possibly the best medicine for those who are often ostracised and criticised for their impulsive actions. Rose Quartz calms, supports and heals emotional wounds, reminding us to be kind to ourselves, while drawing us out of the head and back into the heart.

Citrine adds to this sense by channelling positivity, creativity and self-confidence. It helps us find light and joy at times of darkness. Incidentally, it is also a stone for vitality and energy, so, if all this Citrine is too stimulating for your partner, then replace the Citrine points with Amethyst points to tone down the energy of this layout.

Finally, at the Sacral Chakra, we have Hematite, which is usually placed on the Root Chakra, but, for those with excessive stimulation in their energy, it can be moved higher up.

Hematite works here to provide strong grounding, stability and vibrational weight. It is an excellent stone for the mind, because it promotes focus and concentration, helping to anchor chaotic thoughts.

EXPERT TIPS

◊   Replace the Citrine points with Amethyst points if your partner is hyperactive.

◊   For even more grounding, give your partner a tumbled Hematite stone to hold in each palm throughout this session. (This will help to calm down busy hands too!)

A PERSONAL NOTE

I would love to add that people with ADHD are often exceptionally kinaesthetic and have heightened sensory abilities. My son was diagnosed with ADHD at the age of six and has always sought out extrasensory stimulation. This included having a natural affinity for crystals from a young age.

When he was little, he adored Amethyst, and would wear it on a necklace and keep a little pile of Amethyst crystals under his pillow. He would instantly feel calmer when he held a piece, and he had a little crystal collection on his desk at school too.

Although he couldn't sit still for 3 seconds without bouncing and wriggling around, he would always be able to lie still for a 15-minute crystal treatment. Never underestimate the subtle power of a crystal, a good intention and some healing touch to transform a life!

DEPRESSION

HEALING OUTCOMES

Identification and release of negative thoughts and
programming | Identification and release of a victim mentality |
Healing support through emotionally and mentally challenging
times | Healing support through mild depression and/or anxiety
| A more positive outlook

DIFFICULTY LEVEL

Advanced

CRYSTAL PLACEMENT

EARTH:	Smoky Quartz
HIGHER CROWN:	Purple Fluorite
CROWN:	Sodalite
THIRD EYE:	Turquoise
HEART:	Rose Quartz
SOLAR PLEXUS:	Citrine
SACRAL:	Tiger's Eye
ROOT:	Smoky Quartz

CRYSTAL POINTS

» 2–4 Clear Quartz points placed around the top of the head,
pointing away from the head.

» 2–4 Amethyst points placed around the top of the head,
pointing down towards the head.

» 2 Clear Quartz points placed just below every chakra
(except the Higher Crown). The points should be angled
upwards, a little like an arrowhead, with the tips almost
touching each main chakra crystal.

» 4 Amethyst points placed around and below the Heart Chakra,
pointing in towards the Rose Quartz, all angled in an upwards direction.

» A single Citrine point placed above the Heart Chakra, pointing down towards the chakra. Another Citrine point just below the Sacral Chakra, pointing upwards.

» 2 Citrine points placed either side of the Solar Plexus Chakra, pointing in towards the chakra.

THE HEALING

Sadness, despair and depression carry a very heavy and dark energetic imprint. As such, it is important that we counter this energetic heaviness with a body grid that incorporates lots of high-vibrational crystals.

We should also focus our movements and intentions on channelling the healing energy upwards, connecting to the Crown and Higher Crown chakras. This will help bring a more balanced perspective and lightness to the healing session.

Purple Fluorite at the Higher Crown Chakra stimulates higher consciousness and cleanses the mind of dark and depressive thoughts by casting them into the light. The inwards-facing Amethyst points work by channelling healing, serenity, inner peace and wisdom into the mind. This helps to raise the lower mental vibrations into a higher, more spiritual plane, transforming them into wisdom and understanding.

Clear Quartz around the top of the head works to energetically cleanse and protect against damaging thought processes, such as self-loathing and despair. It does this by releasing low-vibration thoughts and replacing them with clarity. This effect can also help us to recognise chemical imbalances that may be contributing to suboptimal brain functioning.

At the Crown and Third Eye chakras, Sodalite and Turquoise work together to bring calm and cleansing energy. As stones of truth, they encourage honesty with ourselves, while also warding against psychic and psychological attack and paranoia.

Sodalite is particularly useful in calming anxiety and reducing the severity of panic attacks.

Through the Heart and Solar Plexus chakras, Rose Quartz and Citrine (supported by Clear Quartz, Amethyst and Citrine points) resonate with light, joy, love, acceptance, forgiveness, comfort, support and positivity.

You will notice that most of the points in this layout are angled upwards. This is to ensure that the flow of energy is being drawn upwards (away from the heavy, depressive Earth-bound energies) to connect with the high-vibrational light.

Citrine and Rose Quartz make a powerful duo in raising the vibration of any layout. This is especially important when working to transform a profoundly dark and heavy emotional state.

Tiger's Eye at the Sacral Chakra strengthens our sense of self-empowerment and harmonises any dualities that may be contributing to our loss of equilibrium. It protects against all kinds of negative influence and brings strength, insight and courage to an overwhelming situation. Tiger's Eye is reputed to protect against physical and psychological attack, while supporting strength and courage in the face of adversity.

At the Root and Earth chakras, Smoky Quartz grounds and stabilises without being too heavy. It is especially effective in helping energetically to relieve symptoms of depression, negative thoughts and mental anguish.

EXPERT TIPS

◊ Spend extra time charging the chakras in this layout, drawing energy upwards and channelling lots of positive energy into your partner. It is essential to keep connecting the energy of each chakra back to the Higher Crown Chakra.

◊ Direct energy out of the mind by using the Clear Quartz points around the top of the head. Channel calm into the mind by tracing your wand or pendulum along the Amethyst points into the top of the head.

◊ Extra touch by way of Reiki and gentle hand placement over the Heart and Solar Plexus chakras can be exceptionally powerful during this healing. Send your highest love and light intentions into your partner through the palms of your hands.

◊ It can be emotionally, energetically and mentally draining to hold space for, and work with, a partner who is suffering from depression. For this reason, make sure to take appropriate measures to protect yourself and keep your own energy intact. Perform your own protection ritual before and after this session. You may like to cleanse yourself by smudging with white sage or by running a large Selenite (or Smoky Quartz) wand through your aura.

STRENGTH AND COURAGE

HEALING OUTCOMES

Increased self-confidence and courage | Increased emotional and physical strength | Overcoming feelings of insignificance | Reconnecting to our own personal power | Support when feeling stuck or powerless

DIFFICULTY LEVEL

Advanced

CRYSTAL PLACEMENT

EARTH:	Smoky Quartz (upper) and Black Tourmaline (lower)
HIGHER CROWN:	Clear Quartz
THIRD EYE:	Sodalite
THROAT:	Turquoise
HIGHER HEART:	Rose Quartz
HEART:	Malachite
SOLAR PLEXUS:	Tiger's Eye (upper) and Sunstone (lower)
SACRAL:	Orange Agate (or Fire Agate)
ROOT:	Red Garnet

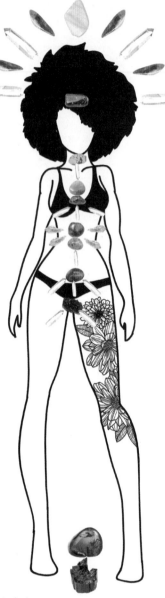

CRYSTAL POINTS

» 2–4 Clear Quartz points placed around the top of the head, pointing away from the head.

» 2–4 Amethyst points placed around the top of the head, pointing down towards the head.

» 2 Clear Quartz points placed just below the Heart, Sacral and Root chakras. The points should be angled upwards, a little like an arrowhead, with the tips almost touching each main chakra crystal.

» A single Clear Quartz point placed between each chakra, pointing upwards towards the Higher Crown Chakra.

» 4 Citrine points placed around the Solar Plexus Chakra, pointing in towards the chakra.

THE HEALING

Courage and strength are powerful energies that we feel with most intensity through the Solar Plexus and Sacral chakras and, to a slightly lesser degree, the Root Chakra.

The Sacral Chakra can be considered the seat of our personal power. It is through this chakra that we connect to our Ego self and our sense of place and strength in the world. It is also where our 'fight or flight' instinct generates, because this chakra connects us to our physical body and survival instinct.

The Solar Plexus Chakra, on the other hand, is the centre through which we feel confidence, inspiration, creativity and vitality. These are the states from which strength and power can blossom. A person who is energetic, confident and inspired is much more likely to have a strong sense of personal power than a person who is lethargic, unmotivated and shy.

To cultivate full-power courage and strength in life, it is important to have a strong sense of connection to our foundation and identity (through the Root and Earth chakras).

Taking all this into account, this layout focuses very much on strengthening and amplifying all the lower chakras with healing stones that are not only powerful, but also provide enough support to underpin the higher chakras too.

This includes the Heart Chakra (for emotional strength), the Throat Chakra (for the courage to speak your truth) and the Third Eye and Crown chakras (for the courage to be true to yourself).

If we look at this layout from the Earth upwards, we begin with Black Tourmaline and Smoky Quartz at the Earth Chakra. Both these stones are used for providing grounding and protection, in addition to being very effective in helping us face and release our deepest fears.

True courage is not defined by the inability to feel fear. It means taking courageous action *despite* feeling fear. It is not courageous to ride an elevator if you are not afraid of small spaces. But it takes great courage if you are claustrophobic!

Through the Root and Sacral chakras, Red Garnet and Orange Agate work together to bring strength and balance to these important energy centres. They help to 'recharge the batteries' and restore vitality to our entire energy system. If these chakras are depleted or weak, then we can find ourselves lacking in motivation and physical strength. However, once we have replenished these energy centres, we are able to draw on our energy reserves when we need them most.

Red Garnet is also a great activator of kundalini energy, which flows upwards through the body, fuelling our chakra system with vitality.

At the Solar Plexus Chakra, Tiger's Eye, Sunstone and Citrine pack a powerful punch! All these stones are dynamite when working on confidence, power and strength. They open the Solar Plexus Chakra for light and energy to flow through, which quickly dissolves feelings of worthlessness, depression, victimisation and despair. Together, they act a bit like a triple-shot espresso for the energy system. They zap us into action, while also offering us the courage and clarity we need to act decisively.

Emotional fear can prevent us from experiencing fulfilling relationships and from pursuing our greatest desires, so the Heart Chakra becomes possibly the most important chakra we need to honour in this layout.

A strong Heart Chakra will help us generate the emotional courage we need to love freely and completely, while living our life with passion and fulfilment, and it is synonymous with bravery and courage.

Malachite is one of the more dynamic heart stones. It penetrates quickly and deeply into the emotional layers to bring forward any heart-trauma that may be holding us back emotionally.

The intensity of Malachite is softened and supported by Rose Quartz at the Higher Heart Chakra, which works to bring understanding, balance and acceptance to the emotions. Together, these two stones energetically heal and support the Heart Chakra, so we can experience emotional strength and stamina.

Turquoise is a stone that has been favoured by Native American peoples for centuries. It is believed to contain powerful healing properties, including the power to bring communication and expression to its wearer, as well as protection.

When placed at the Throat Chakra, Turquoise helps us find the courage to speak our truth and express ourselves authentically, which can sometimes feel like the scariest thing in the world!

Often when we are fearful or find ourselves lacking in courage, it is because we have become disconnected from our purpose and our Higher Self. We feel lost, weak and unsure of ourselves. Perhaps we have even allowed others to dominate us, or simply surrendered our power and survived by drifting along as passive observers of our own life. This is where clarity, refocusing and returning to our spiritual connection are vital.

Sodalite, Clear Quartz and Amethyst resonate with these qualities. They work beautifully alongside one another to cleanse the mind and inspire mental fortitude.

Amethyst also brings calm and serenity, while opening the higher chakras to connect with Spirit. It reminds us that we are infinitely powerful beings, capable of greatness, and that we have the power within ourselves to achieve anything!

EXPERT TIPS

◊   Take your partner through a guided visualisation that includes the colour yellow or gold (such as orbs of golden light). When working with power and courage, it is always best to channel warm colours. Red and orange are also good choices.

◊   Spend extra time charging the chakras, drawing energy upwards and channelling lots of positive energy into your partner. It is essential to keep connecting the energy of the powerful Sacral and Solar Plexus chakras to the Higher Crown Chakra.

◊   Garnet can be substituted with Ruby, and Sunstone can be substituted with Pyrite in this layout.

◊   Remember to cleanse Malachite after each session. While it is excellent at absorbing negative energy, it is not great at converting it into light energy. This means it can hold and store the unwanted energies from one session then release them during the next. Cleanse your Malachite by placing it under a full moon or smudging with palo santo or white sage.

DIRECTION

HEALING OUTCOMES

Clarity seeing the path ahead | Direction and guidance | Assistance in reconnecting with our purpose | Support through feelings of uselessness or inertia | Assistance in determining the next step | Support for getting 'back on track'

DIFFICULTY LEVEL

Advanced

CRYSTAL PLACEMENT

EARTH:	Orthoceras (upper) and Black Tourmaline (lower)
HIGHER CROWN:	Selenite
CROWN:	Clear Quartz
THIRD EYE:	Iolite
HIGHER HEART:	Labradorite
HEART:	Amazonite
SOLAR PLEXUS:	Citrine (upper) and Chiastolite (lower)
SACRAL:	Red Jasper
ROOT:	Chiastolite

CRYSTAL POINTS

» 2–4 Clear Quartz points placed around the top of the head, pointing away from the head.
» 2–4 Amethyst points placed around the top of the head, pointing down towards the head.
» 2–4 Clear Quartz points placed around the Heart, Solar Plexus, Sacral and Root chakras, all pointing in towards the chakras. Half of the points should be angled upwards and half should be angled downwards.
» 4 Citrine points around the Solar Plexus Chakra, pointing in towards the chakra. Make sure at least two of these are angled upwards.

THE HEALING

Haven't we all experienced that feeling of being 'lost' at some point in our lives? It might have been triggered by the loss of a loved one, a relationship break-up, a change of career or just a feeling of dissatisfaction or lack of fulfilment. During these times, the path ahead suddenly becomes unclear. We might find ourselves overwhelmed by feelings of uncertainty, confusion or even paralysis, as we are frozen in our present state, unsure of what to do next.

Whatever the cause of these feelings, it is important to remember that there is always a positive path forward.

When someone is feeling lost it is because the two most important anchor points have become blocked or temporarily disconnected. These are the Earth and Higher Crown chakras.

Safety, security and strong foundations all come through the Earth Chakra. So, when the proverbial rug is swept out from beneath our feet (such as when a long-term relationship falls apart), it causes a massive destabilisation to our sense of safety, security and foundation. This is like an earthquake to the Earth Chakra, which rocks our entire energy system and throws everything off-balance.

For this reason, we use Black Tourmaline and Orthoceras at the Earth Chakra in this layout. Both these stones provide a deep sense of security and grounding.

Orthoceras is particularly important and should not be substituted, because it is the stone that connects us most powerfully to our ancestral and earthly history. It can be impossible to step with trust and confidence into the future if we do not own or connect with our past. Because it is strong and protective, Black Tourmaline is a great additional choice and provides us with that much-needed sense of safety as we look towards the unknown.

If we become disconnected from our Higher Self by trauma to the Crown or Higher Crown chakras, then we may find ourselves questioning our purpose and all that is meaningful to us. As such, we use Selenite and Clear Quartz at the Higher Crown and Crown chakras in this layout.

Selenite works to open the higher chakras, strengthening the connection to Spirit and the Higher Self, while Clear Quartz brings cleansing and clarity. Together, these stones help us to approach the future with lucidity, but also with the type of intuitive confidence that comes from knowing we are honouring our Highest Self.

Often when we feel lost, our inner compass becomes unpredictable and erratic. This clouds our vision and affects our ability to decide on the best direction to take. We begin to second-guess ourselves as we flounder and procrastinate over what our next step should be. Iolite at the Third Eye will help to bring everything back into sharp focus, clearing the inner eye's fog, so we can clearly see the options laid out before us.

Incidentally, Iolite is regarded as a powerful shaman's stone because of its ability to open the Third Eye and hone visionary capacity.

At the Higher Heart and Heart chakras, Labradorite and Amazonite work to balance and heal the emotions, while also encouraging wisdom, clarity and understanding.

Labradorite, in its multi-coloured mysticism, helps us to view our situation in a new light and understand it from a deeper perspective. Once we can understand a situation, we can begin to move towards acceptance. This will help us to release the trauma from whatever pushed us off course, so we can find our way back to our soul-path.

At the Solar Plexus Chakra, Citrine holds the energies of light, positivity and confidence. It reminds us that we can create a positive outcome from a confusing or painful situation, trust our instinct and look towards the future with optimism.

As we know from the layouts for 'Transition and change' (see page 140) and for 'Spiritual awakening' (see page 171), Chiastolite is the crossroads stone. At the Solar Plexus Chakra, it brings certainty and direction, helping to repair our inner compass so we can navigate our way forward. It works wonderfully with the energy of Citrine to promote confidence in our decision-making.

Finally, through the lower chakras, we have Red Jasper and more Chiastolite. Both these stones provide excellent grounding and assistance in releasing anything that does not serve us. This means we can move forward freely, feeling unburdened by the past. These stones help us not only to release energetic trauma, but also to 'find our footing' so we can take the next big step.

EXPERT TIPS

◊ Take your partner through a guided visualisation that includes imagining a crossroads intersection with a direction sign that is covered by a thick fog. Ask your partner to visualise peering or walking into the fog until it starts to dissipate. You might even ask your partner to blow the fog away. Encourage your partner to stay in this space until the sign becomes visible and a direction becomes clear.

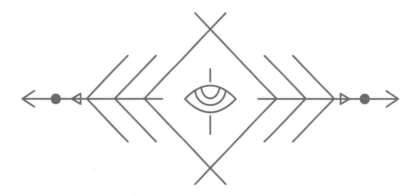

PROTECTION

HEALING OUTCOMES

Physical protection (such as when travelling) | Spiritual and energetic protection (such as from negative influences and projections, spirits or entities, and energetically draining people or situations) | Emotional protection from hurtful people or situations (such as bullying) | Psychological protection (from mental stress-triggers) | Creating a barrier between the Self and the outside world (during times of vulnerability or introspection)

DIFFICULTY LEVEL

Advanced

CRYSTAL PLACEMENT

EARTH:	Black Tourmaline (upper) and large Selenite stick (lower) in a vertical position
HIGHER CROWN:	Large Selenite stick placed in a vertical position
BESIDE EACH ARM:	Large Selenite stick placed outside and beside each arm in a vertical position
THIRD EYE:	Amethyst
HEART:	Malachite
SACRAL:	Smoky Quartz
ROOT:	Smoky Quartz

CRYSTAL POINTS

» 2–4 Amethyst points placed around the top of the head, pointing down towards the head.

» 2–4 Amethyst points placed around the Heart Chakra, pointing in towards the chakra.

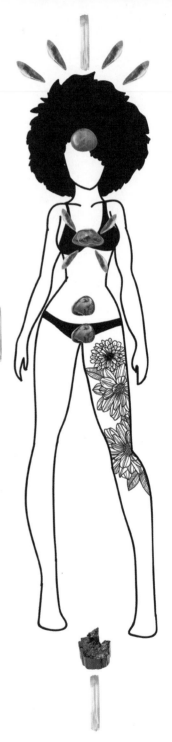

THE HEALING

This healing layout draws on the protective qualities of some of the crystal kingdom's most effective protection stones.

The four-point Selenite layout surrounding the body (beside each arm and at the Higher Crown and Earth chakras) acts as a complete energetic shield.

I have used four pieces of Selenite to honour four cardinal points and four levels of being: physical, psychological, emotional and spiritual. If you have more Selenite on hand, you can place more pieces around the body if it feels right. You may like to place a stick beside each leg or alongside the torso.

Selenite is one of the most powerful spiritual protection stones. It wards off dark entities, spirits and spiritual attack, creating a barrier through which no negative and low-vibrational energy can pass. It is excellent for cleansing and protecting the aura and effective in removing energetic debris that may be clinging to our energy field.

Amethyst at the Third Eye and Higher Crown chakras protects against negative spiritual influences, low-vibrational thoughts and empathic absorption. Empaths are those who unintentionally 'absorb' or 'own' the energies, thoughts and feelings of those around them. Empathic ability can be a wonderful gift with many empaths becoming successful clairvoyants, healers and mediums. However, some have no 'filter', which leaves them unable to be selective as to which energies they absorb.

At the heart, Malachite works to protect, balance and heal the emotions. We know by now that Malachite is not a subtle healer. It will crack open your Heart Chakra and bring buried emotional trauma to the surface, whether you are ready to face it or not! Despite its intensity, Malachite is extremely effective at absorbing negative energy and warding off physical and emotional attack.

The effect of Malachite in this layout is supported and softened by the Amethyst points. These add a more spiritual dimension to the heart-healing, helping us understand any emotional trauma that surfaces within our higher consciousness.

Smoky Quartz works on the lower chakras to protect on a physical level. It also resonates with the psychological body to protect against negative thoughts, depression, anxiety and harmful programming.

Black Tourmaline is possibly the most powerful protection stone in this layout, guarding against trauma on all levels. It is also beneficial because it helps us identify and release our fears.

One could argue that protection is not necessary if we do not attract negative entities through a fear-based vibration. If we exist in a state of fear and worry, then that is the vibration that we send into the world. The Law of Attraction states that like attracts like on an energetic and cosmic level. If we harbour a fear-based vibration within ourselves, then we will energetically attract that which we fear. But if we raise our vibrational state out of fear and into a state of trust and acceptance, we are potentially much less likely to need protection.

EXPERT TIPS

◊ Always thoroughly cleanse Malachite after each use as it tends to store and amplify the energies it absorbs, including the negative ones.

◊ Other effective protection stones that can be incorporated into this layout include Turquoise (at the Third Eye, Throat or Heart chakras), Tiger's Eye (at the Solar Plexus, Sacral or Root chakras) and Black Obsidian (at the Earth Chakra).

CANCER

HEALING OUTCOMES

Cellular support | Energetic support during chemotherapy | Healing support for tumours and cancerous growths | Healing support for states of remission

DIFFICULTY LEVEL

Advanced

CRYSTAL PLACEMENT

EARTH: Smoky Quartz
HIGHER CROWN: Large Selenite stick in a vertical position
BESIDE EACH ARM: Large Selenite stick placed outside and beside
                   each arm in a vertical position
BESIDE EACH KNEE: Large Selenite stick placed outside and beside
                   each knee in a vertical position
CROWN: Clear Quartz
HEART: Malachite
SOLAR PLEXUS: Citrine
ROOT: Smoky Quartz

CRYSTAL POINTS

» Optional: a few Citrine points placed around each chakra, pointing inwards.

THE HEALING

There is no 'one size fits all' approach to a layout that supports healing in the case of cancer, because each person's experience is unique.

Ideally, you would have enough experience and knowledge working with crystals and energy to be able to design a layout that is specific to your partner. However, this layout will offer good, general energetic healing support for those who have or recently have had cancer.

Consider these factors when performing this layout:

◊ the age and physical health of your partner

◊ the nature of the cancer/tumour

◊ the location of the cancer/tumour

◊ the severity and advancement of the cancer/tumour

◊ any treatments your partner is currently receiving (or has previously received).

When performing a crystal healing layout to support those with cancer, it is vital that only safe crystals are used. Safe crystals are those that have exceptional cleansing ability and do not energetically support the growth of tumorous cells.

The selected crystals also need to be effective in drawing out disease and illness, while supporting healing and promoting regeneration in healthy cells.

One such stone is Selenite. Selenite provides a protective shield from dark entities and vibrational states, including illness. Because Selenite is so high-vibe, it is used abundantly in this layout.

Selenite works to raise the vibration of the energetic body to such a high state that it becomes an undesirable environment for low-vibrational cancer cells to flourish. The experience of being elevated to such a heightened state can cause your partner to feel quite light-headed after the session, so it is important to allow adequate time for recovery and grounding.

IMPORTANT

This is highly advanced crystal healing work. Only a small number of crystals are considered safe when working with people who have or recently have had cancer.

Most crystals promote cellular growth on an energetic level, which can be detrimental (rather than beneficial) to health when working with cancerous cells in the body. Unless you are an experienced crystal therapist, it can be difficult, energetically speaking, to distinguish between healthy cells and tumorous cells in the body.

For this reason, please do not substitute any of the crystals in this layout. All the crystals included here are considered safe to use on cancer patients, even if your crystal healing experience is limited.

Smoky Quartz at the Root and Earth chakras provides this grounding without compromising on the high-vibrational energies required of this layout.

Smoky Quartz is regarded as being effective at filtering electromagnetic pollution. This makes it a great choice when cleansing and healing the energetic body after radiation or chemotherapy treatment. It also helps us in releasing fear, which is helpful for a person facing such an uncertain future.

Malachite is one of the most powerful absorbers of illness and low-vibrational energy in the mineral kingdom. It acts like an energetic sponge, sucking up debris, fear, anger and illness from the energetic body. It also works to provide energetic protection from illness and injury, as well as much-needed emotional support for the Heart Chakra.

As is always important (and even more so here), please remember to cleanse your Malachite stone thoroughly after each use, as it does not transmute dark energy into light. Rather, in keeping with its sponge-like characteristics, it holds onto what it has absorbed and needs to be 'wrung out' after each use. See the 'Expert tips' section below for how to do this.

To help transmute low-vibrational illness into health, we include Citrine at the Solar Plexus Chakra and Clear Quartz at the Crown Chakra.

Positive emotions such as confidence, self-esteem and optimism are more readily available to us when the Solar Plexus Chakra is charged. That is why we use Citrine here, as it provides us with the favourable energy we need to find the light in even the most despairing of situations.

Clear Quartz is possibly the most powerful healer and cleanser of all the crystals. It works on all levels to unblock and release non-serving energy and replace it with optimal energetic health. This is important when working on a cellular level to provide the right kind of vibrational nourishment for healthy cells to thrive.

EXPERT TIPS

◊ Make sure you thoroughly cleanse Malachite after each use to release any negative energy and illness it has absorbed. My preferred cleansing methods include smudging with white sage or placing the stone out under a full moon overnight.

MANIFESTATION

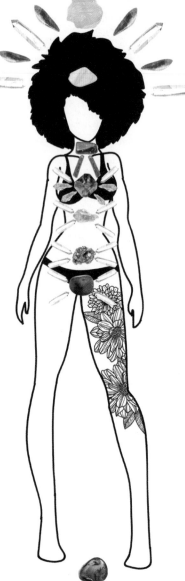

HEALING OUTCOMES

Manifesting and attracting a soulmate | Manifesting abundance and wealth | Manifesting your dream life and career | Attracting life's opportunities | Manifesting a specific outcome or scenario

DIFFICULTY LEVEL

Advanced

CRYSTAL PLACEMENT

EARTH:	Smoky Quartz
HIGHER CROWN:	Clear Calcite
CROWN:	Clear Quartz
THROAT:	Sodalite
HEART:	Emerald
SOLAR PLEXUS:	Citrine
SACRAL:	Pyrite
ROOT:	Bloodstone

CRYSTAL POINTS

» 2–4 Amethyst points placed around the top of the head, pointing down towards the head.

» 2–4 Clear Quartz points placed around the top of the head, pointing away from the head.

» 2 Kyanite blades placed either side and just below the Throat Chakra, pointing in towards the throat.

» 2 Clear Quartz points placed either side and slightly above the Heart, Solar Plexus, Sacral and Root chakras, pointing in towards each chakra and angled downwards.

» 2 Clear Quartz points placed either side and slightly below the Heart, Solar Plexus, Sacral and Root chakras, pointing in towards each chakra and angled upwards.

» 4–6 Citrine points placed around the Heart Chakra, pointing in towards the heart.

ELEMENTS OF MANIFESTATION

When working with manifestation, there are a few key elements we need to master to achieve true success in realising our goals.

CLARITY

We need to be perfectly clear about what outcome we want to manifest. Be precise and specific with any requests, and visualise as much detail as possible. The universe can only deliver if our vision and message is crystal clear.

Let's say you want to manifest more money. To do so, don't focus your manifestation on 'more money'. This is not specific enough. Also, this type of intention comes from a belief state of lack (see 'Attitude of gratitude' below). By not being specific and setting your intention as simply attracting 'more money', the universe does not know how to accurately deliver on your request. You may cross the road and find a $5 note on the street one day (which is technically 'more money'), but this is almost certainly not what you had in mind!

Instead, visualise the new car or the holiday you want the money for. Specify an exact amount you desire to attract as well as a timeframe for when you want to have it by. This way you are sending out a clear energetic vibration, which the universe can respond to more accurately.

ATTITUDE OF GRATITUDE

Any time we set our minds to attracting or manifesting something in our lives, the intention must come from a place of gratitude. In other words, we must frame our request in an abundance mindset, rather than a mindset of lack or feeling 'less than'.

Have you ever found yourself stressed about money? How many of us have been guilty of saying 'I don't have enough money' or 'I can't afford it'? These thoughts and words are damaging and, when repeated often enough, send that exact message to the universe. It becomes self-perpetuating.

The more you feel you are lacking, the more this 'lack energy' is amplified by the universe. The universe delivers on your request. So, when we are trying to manifest something, it is vital that the request is framed in an abundant, gratitude-filled way.

Rather than dismissing an opportunity because you 'don't have enough money', try telling yourself instead that the money is 'on its way'. And instead of asking for 'more money' (which comes from an energy of lack or not having enough), ask the

universe how you can grow the abundance you already have. This philosophy does not only apply to money, but to everything in life!

PATIENCE IS KEY

The universe works to a completely different schedule from the one we live by. Although you may be tempted to feel frustrated and disappointed when you don't see immediate results, it is important to stick with your intention. Don't give up if your goal is not achieved immediately, or in a week, or even in a year. Trust it will manifest and present itself to you when the time is right.

THE HEALING

Now that we understand the type of mindset and vibrational state we need to foster in order to manifest successfully, we can better understand the crystals used in this layout.

Clear Calcite and Clear Quartz at the higher chakras bring clarity to our vision, helping us define our goals with precision. They work to clear the mind of any belief systems and blockages that may be sabotaging our success and preventing our goals from manifesting.

Clear Calcite also acts as a doorway between the worlds, clearing the path for Divine inspiration and Spirit to flow through.

Clear Quartz is programmable, which means it can be worked with to imprint our own specific outcomes and desires into the stone for greater manifestation capabilities.

At the Throat Chakra, we use Sodalite and Kyanite. These stones help us to express our deepest desires clearly, but also with integrity. Remember, we want to avoid using language that comes from a low-vibrational state of greed, lack or ingratitude. This includes our inner dialogue in the form of thoughts.

Kyanite greatly supports this, enabling us to communicate with truth, integrity and the essence of our Higher Self. This ensures our most authentic message is received by the universe.

At the Heart Chakra, we use Emerald. Being one of the four precious stones (along with Diamond, Ruby and Sapphire), it is a stone of rarity, abundance and value. If Emerald is unavailable, another green stone of excellent clarity is recommended.

It is important to select a clear stone at the Heart Chakra in this layout to communicate clearly with the universe about our heart's desires. We want complete emotional transparency, which eliminates confusion and uncertainty, so that we can attract what we truly desire.

At the same time, this emotional clarity reveals our truest desires to ourselves. Sometimes we think we want something (such as the love of an emotionally abusive partner). However, if we can connect with our clearest, purest and most authentic Self, we can see that this is not truly what we desire (or deserve) after all.

Through the Solar Plexus and Sacral chakras, we use Citrine and Pyrite, which are powerful, abundance-manifesting stones.

Both stones work to align the lower chakras physically with our vibrational state. This means that not only can we manifest emotional and mental states such as confidence, opportunity, personal power and positivity with success, but we can use these states to attract tangible outcomes such as more wealth, a new job and physical objects (such as a new car or house).

When the lower chakras are strong and aligned, we are more able to tap into our inner source of power and greatness. We are then capable of achieving amazing things that may previously have seemed impossible!

Bloodstone works at the Root Chakra to cleanse and detoxify. It also helps to bring into our awareness anything that has been sabotaging our path towards success.

Being such an effective cleansing stone, Bloodstone helps us to purge ourselves energetically of non-serving belief patterns, physical dependencies and negative mindsets (including ingratitude and any victimhood).

This cleansing effect is amplified by Smoky Quartz at the Earth Chakra. Smoky Quartz helps bring awareness to our own self-destructive behaviour and transmutes negativity into a more positive mindset, which is essential for manifestation work. It helps us to ground, reset and focus, so that we can identify opportunities around us that will best serve our evolutionary path.

EXPERT TIPS

◊ Visualisation is one of the most powerful tools when working with manifestation. Ask your partner to describe to you what their desired outcome looks like, smells like, feels like and so on. When working with visualisation, it is essential that we get a sense of not only what the desired outcome would look like, but what it would feel like now. If we are visualising an outcome at some point in the future, without feeling its effect on us in real time, then energetically this is just like experiencing a daydream. It may look nice in our mind's eye, but it doesn't have much effect on our vibrational state. When we imagine how the outcome feels now (and can truly immerse ourselves in this feeling on an energetic level), then our entire vibrational state will change. We become much more energetically aligned with the desired outcome and the universe will match this vibrational frequency. Opportunities that were previously invisible to us will suddenly present themselves and things will begin to shift in a new direction.

FROM ONE SPIRITUAL REBEL TO ANOTHER

As a Spiritual Rebel, it is your prerogative to find your own path of spiritual evolution in a way that resonates uniquely with you. Keep in mind that this may be quite different from everyone else's journey, and that's awesome!

To help you to get the most from this book and your broader spiritual healing journey as you evolve, it is essential that you remain authentic in your practice, working in a way that honours your true spiritual Self.

Spiritual teachers, gurus and experts can provide you with the direction and guidance you need to progress at each stage, but never compromise on your authenticity or spiritual integrity for someone else's idea of what your journey should look like.

It is perfectly okay to question, challenge and not fit the norm (even if that means rocking up to a yoga retreat on a Harley-Davidson or choosing roast chicken over tofu).

Finally, if you take only one message from this book, I would like it to be this: trust yourself when working with your crystals, because healing is just as much about listening to and honouring your inner voice as using effective technique.

Begin every crystal healing from your place of highest intention and focus your attention on where you feel most called. If you stop and listen, you *will* hear the answers. It is amazing what you can achieve when you learn to trust your intuition!

From one Spiritual Rebel to another … I wish you heartfelt abundance, joy and inspiration on your healing journey.

INDEX OF CRYSTAL BODY LAYOUTS

ABOUT THE AUTHOR

Kate Mantello is a Master Energy Healer, creator of the 'Transpersonal Crystal Healing' modality and founder of Evolve Healing Institute, a world-class international training platform for crystal and energy healing practitioners. Since its launch in early 2017, Evolve Healing Institute has delivered over 20,000 online crystal healing courses and trained over 1000 certified crystal healing practitioners all around the world.

As a lifelong Spiritual Rebel, Kate has always lived life by her own rules. She is passionate about personal development and has learned to trust her intuition and be courageous when it comes to following her true path.

When she is not writing, teaching and presenting, she can be found rocking out to 90s grunge, sweating at the gym and enjoying life on the Sunshine Coast with her Canadian-bear hubby and two feral free-spirited kids, who also happen to be her greatest teachers.

KATEMANTELLO.COM | EVOLVEHEALING.NET

ACKNOWLEDGEMENTS

This book is the culmination of more than a decade of work and would not have been possible without the trust and support from the following beautiful people. A huge and heartfelt thank you to:

Lisa Hanrahan, for believing in this book enough to let me pitch to her on-the-job in Brisbane. I appreciate this opportunity from the bottom of my heart!

Sara Lindberg and the design team at Rockpool who have outdone themselves in bringing my vision to life with such a stunning offering.

Alex, Kris and Gabiann, for your invaluable editing advice, feedback and suggestions. You took this rough gemstone and polished it into something dazzling!

My cousin Jane, for her wisdom and advice when I needed it.

And finally, my deepest gratitude and love to Rob, Sol and Edie. Your unwavering faith in me is humbling. I couldn't have done this without you.

A Rockpool book
PO Box 252
Summer Hill
NSW 2130
Australia

rockpoolpublishing.co
Follow us! **f** ⓘ rockpoolpublishing
Tag your images with #rockpoolpublishing

ISBN: 9781925946543

Published in 2021 by Rockpool Publishing
Copyright text © Kate Mantello 2021
Copyright design © Rockpool Publishing
Copyright images (on p. iv, 7, 80, 95 3rd image, 242–243)
© Kate Mantello 2021

Other images from Shutterstock, unsplash and pixabay
Design by Sara Lindberg, Rockpool Publishing
Edited by Alexandra Payne

DISCLAIMER

Crystal healing is a complementary healing modality and
does not replace proper medical care, nor is it a suitable
stand-alone treatment for any injury, illness or medical
condition you or someone you know may have (including
mental illness).

The information provided in this book is not intended
to be used as a substitute for medical or psychological
treatment. Under no circumstances should prescribed
medical treatment (including prescription medications)
be halted unless your licensed medical professional has
instructed you to do so. We accept no responsibility for
the actions and choices made by the reader, in response
to the information, practices and treatments described
herein.

Kate Mantello is a fully qualified and experienced
Transpersonal Therapist and Crystal Healing
Practitioner. She practises under a strict code of ethics
and encourages readers of this book to do the same.
Kate Mantello accepts no liability or responsibility for
any readers who fail to adhere to this code of ethics,
including (but not limited to) practising the techniques
described herein, within the limits of their qualifications
and experience.

NATIONAL
LIBRARY
OF AUSTRALIA

A catalogue record for this
book is available from the
National Library of Australia

Printed and bound in China
10 9 8 7 6 5 4 3 2 1

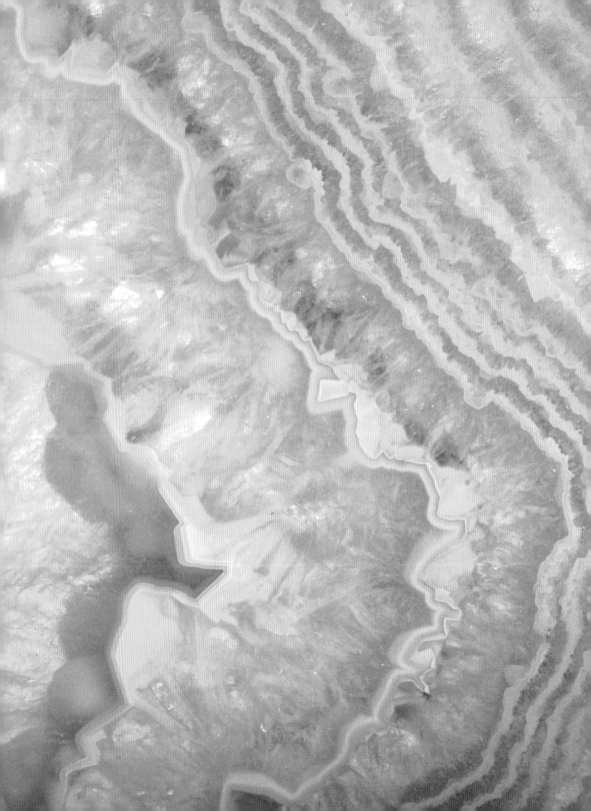